AT HOME WITH THE AZTECS

At Home with the Aztecs provides a fresh view of Aztec society, focusing on households and communities instead of kings, pyramids, and human sacrifice. This new approach offers an opportunity to humanize the Aztecs, moving past the popular stereotype of sacrificial maniacs, to demonstrate that these were successful and prosperous communities. Michael Smith also engagingly describes the scientific, logistic, and personal dimensions of archaeological fieldwork, drawing on decades of excavating experience and considering how his research was affected by his interaction with contemporary Mexican communities. Through first-hand accounts of the ways archaeologists interpret sites and artifacts, the book illuminates how the archaeological process can provide information about ancient families. Facilitating a richer understanding of the Aztec world, Smith's research also redefines success, prosperity, and resilience in ancient societies, making this book suitable not only for those interested in the Aztecs but in the examination of complex societies in general.

Michael E. Smith is one of the leading international authorities on the Aztecs, with extensive experience excavating Aztec sites. He is currently a Professor of Anthropology in the School of Human Evolution and Social Change at Arizona State University.

AT HOME WITH THE AZTECS

An archaeologist uncovers their daily life

Michael E. Smith

LONDON AND NEW YORK

First published 2016
by Routledge
2 Park Square, Milton Park, Abingdon, Oxon OX14 4RN

and by Routledge
711 Third Avenue, New York, NY 10017

Routledge is an imprint of the Taylor & Francis Group, an informa business

British Library Cataloguing-in-Publication Data
A catalogue record for this book is available from the British Library

Library of Congress Cataloging-in-Publication Data
A catalog record for this book has been requested

ISBN: 978-1-138-10075-6 (hbk)
ISBN: 978-1-138-10074-9 (pbk)
ISBN: 978-1-315-65750-9 (ebk)

Typeset in Bembo Std
by Swales & Willis Ltd, Exeter, Devon, UK

Printed and bound by CPI Group (UK) Ltd, Croydon, CR0 4YY

I dedicate this book to the *campesinos* of the Mexican state of Morelos: the farmers whose story I tell and their descendants who helped me uncover that story.

CONTENTS

FIGURES

PREFACE

Any archaeological project requires the contributions of many people. Here I will mention only the key participants in the research described in this book. Full lists of our Mexican workers and all of the students and colleagues who participated in some way can be found in the excavation reports, listed in the bibliography. My able student supervisors at Capilco and Cuexcomate were Patricia Aguirre, Kris Hirst, and Scott O'Mack. Martín Antonio, Jeff Price and Osvaldo Sterpone also excavated for part of the season. Jeff assisted with site mapping in 1985, and my brother Smitty spent a few days swatting bugs and mapping with us. My wife Cindy, who appears frequently in the pages of this book, was an excavation supervisor at these sites and again at Yautepec. She helped train the students on both projects. Cheryl Sutherland was our lab supervisor during the Capilco and Cuexcomate excavations, and Susan Goodfellow, Kathleen Haynie, Colleen Rhodes, Jerrel Sorensen, and Deborah Szymborski all worked in the lab (as did Cindy, of course). April and Heather Smith also helped out during the fieldwork and lab seasons, in ways that only small girls can. Our friends and compadres in Tetlama made our stays in Mexico enjoyable and satisfying, and we thank them for their support and friendship over the years (and for the mole).

Fieldworkers on the urban survey at Yautepec were Cindy, Ronald Kohler, Joan Odess, Sharon Spanogle, Timothy Sullivan, and myself. The graduate student excavation supervisors on the Yautepec excavations were Ruth Fauman-Fichman, Lisa Montiel, Susan Norris, and Margaret Shiels, with assistance from undergraduates Robert Austin, Nili Badanowski, Elizabeth DiPippo, and Brian Tomasewski. Lab work and analyses were performed by Wendy Feiock, Timothy Hare, Joshua Hatton, Dorothy Hosler, Benjamin Karis, Kori Kaufman, Anita López, Annette MacLeod, Lisa Montiel, Jan Marie Olson, Susan Norris, Lea Pickard, Jennifer

Pinson, Geoffrey Purcell, David Schafer, Jay Silverstein, Brian Tomaszewski, Jennifer Wharton, and Richard Wilkinson.

This research was funded primarily by grants from the Archaeology Program at the National Science Foundation. Additional support came from Loyola University, the University at Albany (SUNY), the National Geographic Society, the Heinz Foundation, the National Endowment for the Humanities, our own family budget, and the Dudley B. Smith "Pickup trucks for Mike" fund.

Many officials and colleagues in Mexico contributed to the success of these projects. I am especially grateful for the help, advice, and friendship of Norberto González, Silvia Garza, and Hortensia de Vega Nova in Cuernavaca. The entire staff of the Centro INAH Morelos in Cuernavaca contributed in many ways to this research. I want to acknowledge the assistance of Norberto González and Joaquin García-Bárcena in their roles as director of the Consejo de Arqueología of the Instituto Nacional de Antropología e Historia in Mexico City.

Several citizens of Yautepec were particularly helpful to the project. Members of the Peña family provided our laboratory in Yautepec and assisted in many ways over the years. I especially thank María de la Concepción Peña Flores for her support of our work in Yautepec. Her sister Judith has also been very helpful. We are grateful for the help and friendship of the entire Peña Flores family. Raúl and Rosa Galindo aided us greatly during the Yautepec survey. César Ortiz has been a good friend, personally and professionally. In Cuernavaca the Leguízamo family (and their German shepherds, Harry and Tanagra) provided a home away from home for us, and honorary Mexican grandparents for April and Heather.

This has been the most "fun" book I have written. I incurred many debts during the process. My agent, Barbara Braun, showed faith in the project and helped me to get the manuscript into shape. My writing coach, Leslie Rubinski (of the Creative Nonfiction Mentors program) taught me how to write narrative text that someone besides an archaeologist might want to read. Cindy edited several passages of the book, but most helpful has been her editing of many of my works over the years. When I am poised to write some currently trendy term, I hear her voice in my head saying "That's jargon!" I thank the following friends, family, and colleagues for providing very helpful feedback on key passages of the book: Bradford Andrews, Frances Berdan, Heather Griffith, Cynthia Heath-Smith, Michelle Hegmon, Dorothy Hosler, Peggy Nelson, and Chris Morehart.

This book was written during a sabbatical leave from Arizona State University. Cindy's parents, James and Maxine Heath, let me stay in their home for a month of writing and dog-sitting. I also benefitted from a few weeks in residence at the Amerind Foundation, in 2012 and 2014, thanks to John Ware. Public lectures at the Amerind Foundation, the Maya Society of Minnesota, and Pacific Lutheran University helped me organize my thoughts about these sites and their story.

A visit to the Lowell Milken Center for Unsung Heroes in Fort Scott, Kansas, stimulated my thinking on the larger importance of the faceless ancient Aztec farmers whose lives I try to reconstruct in this book. I thank Kagan McLeod for his excellent illustrations that bring ancient Aztec communities to life.

My family has been a source of support and inspiration, beginning with the trips Cindy and I made to Cuernavaca as graduate students, continuing through numerous drives to Mexico with April and Heather in the back seat, and continuing today in many ways.

1

RUSTY NAILS, STONE WALLS, AND A DRUM

The first sign that something was wrong was when a student excavator called me over to see what looked like a rusty nail she had just excavated from an Aztec house. Iron artifacts are typical at historical and recent sites in Mexico—but not deep in Aztec-period trash deposits. The peoples of Mexico did not have iron technology before Cortés arrived in 1519 to conquer the Aztec Empire. A few days later a different excavator—my wife, Cynthia Heath-Smith—found a similar artifact that looked like a piece of stiff copper wire. We sat down in the shade to examine this wire or nail carefully.

"This thing is covered with layers of corrosion," she said, "but it doesn't look like rust."

"Look. Here, where it's chipped."

"Yes, it has the color of copper or bronze, not iron. This can't be a nail."

"I'll have Kris tell her workers to be more careful not to damage artifacts during excavation."

"But that isn't the point! See how one end is pointed and the other has a small hole? This is a sewing needle, and it must be made of copper or bronze! And it came out of an Aztec trash deposit!"

Cindy was right. This object turned out to be a sewing needle, not a nail or wire at all! And tests later showed it to be made of bronze, not iron or copper (Figure 1.1). That solved the problem of modern iron objects in an Aztec site (there were none), but introduced a deeper mystery of its own.

It was 1986 and we were beginning excavations in the Aztec village of Capilco, not far from the modern city of Cuernavaca in Mexico. I had chosen this site for my first excavation after receiving my Ph.D. because I wanted to find out what life was like for Aztec farmers. As a small and isolated village far away from any major

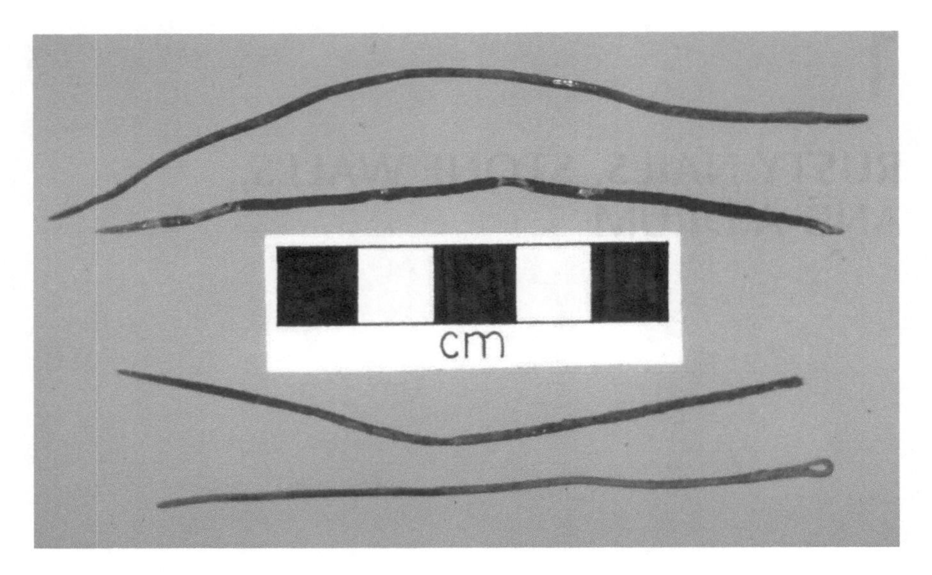

FIGURE 1.1 Bronze needles from Capilco. Photograph by Michael E. Smith.

cities, located in an area conquered by the Mexica or Aztec Empire, Capilco sat at the bottom of the Aztec social hierarchy. Therefore, I reasoned, these Aztec peasants should not have owned or used things made of bronze. This was one of the most sophisticated technologies of ancient Mexico. Bronze tools and ritual items were manufactured in the Tarascan Empire of western Mexico and traded to the Aztec realm, and they were highly valuable items. Most of the surviving examples had come from ceremonial offerings at Tenochtitlan, the Aztec imperial capital (buried under Mexico City today).

In the two months we dug at Capilco more bronze items turned up. Besides the needles, we uncovered some small bells, a couple of awls or punches, and a few other items. I was totally unprepared for these finds. An expert in Aztec pottery analysis (at least I thought so upon completing my Ph.D.), I had researched the kinds of artifacts we were likely to find at these sites: knives made from the volcanic glass obsidian, grinding tools made from basalt rock, animal bones, and the like. But bronze? The possibility that we might find such artifacts at a site like Capilco had not even crossed my mind. I wrote to my friend Dr. Dorothy Hosler at the Massachusetts Institute of Technology, the leading expert on ancient Mexican bronze technology, and asked her how to handle our artifacts. She got excited and arranged to fly down at the end of the field season to see them. Dorothy later did a full scientific analysis, and our collection of bronze artifacts turned out to be extremely important for understanding the technology and trade of bronze in ancient Mexico. But these finds really puzzled me. What were these exotic and valuable imported goods doing in a small rural village?

The second mystery that season consisted of irregular rows of stone on the hillsides surrounding Cuexcomate, a larger site three kilometers from Capilco. When we finished excavating at Capilco, I moved our crew to this new site. Houses at Cuexcomate were spread along the top of a ridge surrounded by rocky slopes. We had walked all over these slopes for weeks when a newly arrived student, Osvaldo Sterpone, came up to talk with me.

"Look at that slope over there," he said, "The one with all the rocks."

"Yes? All the fields around here are full of rocks." I had twisted my ankle on one of these loose stones, and I was not thrilled about the rocks spread all over the place.

"But over there, it looks like some of the rocks are arranged in parallel rows. Could these be the remains of ancient agricultural terraces?"

We walked over to take a closer look. When we got close, I saw it immediately: horizontal rows of rocks, one after another, running down the slope. Osvaldo was right. These hillsides had once been covered with the stone walls of agricultural terraces. Many of the walls had collapsed, sending stones rolling down the hill and leaving only traces of the original terrace lines. Cuexcomate turned out to be both surrounded by, and filled with, agricultural terrace fields. The extent of these fields was almost as puzzling as the bronze tools. I asked myself why they needed so many walled fields. Terracing is a form of intensive agriculture, a type of farming that requires considerable labor, skills, and coordination. Why would a provincial town like Cuexcomate require this level of investment in farming?

As excavations continued at Cuexcomate, a third puzzle presented itself in the form of an amorphous pile of rocks. We had noticed rock piles near some of the houses. Osvaldo Sterpone was doing his excavation practicum on the project, which meant he needed to spend four weeks excavating as part of his training at the Mexican National School of Archaeology. I assigned him a rock pile to excavate, figuring he couldn't do much harm clearing off a bunch of rocks that probably meant nothing. But the rocks turned out to be a ceremonial deposit created as part of the Aztec New Fire Ceremony—and Osvaldo turned out to be an excellent archaeologist. He excavated the rock pile with skill and his maps and notes were first-rate. This feature is one of the few archaeological finds proving the Aztec peoples did indeed celebrate the possible end of the world every fifty-two years. But that wasn't the only mystery of this rock pile.

Another puzzling thing was the strange pot we were able to glue together (back in the lab) from sherds, or pot fragments, that Osvaldo excavated under the rocks. It was clear that someone had taken a bunch of ceramic vessels and deliberately thrown them into a big pile where they broke into fragments. While this sounds like fun to me, the people who broke these pots were carrying out a ceremony. The heap of pot fragments sat under the layer of rocks, and the first broken pot to emerge from excavation was an unusual jar-like object. Big pottery expert that I thought I was, it took me several years to identify this thing, and it remains one of the strangest objects I have ever excavated. It was a ceramic drum, used in ceremonies. I didn't identify it as a drum at first, but I figured it probably had a special ceremonial purpose. It did not look anything like Aztec cooking or storage pots.

There is an archaeological joke suggesting that whenever we find some strange artifact we can't figure out, we say that it must have been a ritual object.

Most archaeologists think they are too sophisticated to interpret unusual artifacts this way—rigorous archaeologists don't think like that. In fact, this joke is closer to the truth than many of us would like to admit. That odd ceramic vessel didn't fit any standard category, so I concluded that it must have been a ritual object. When I finally determined that the object was a drum, my ceremonial interpretation turned out to be correct. But at the time of excavation, the idea that some kind of sophisticated ritual drum was used at Cuexcomate, and then discarded in a big ceremonial dump, seemed unlikely. Why did the provincial peoples at this small Aztec town have such a fancy object? And why did they break it deliberately?

These three mysteries—bronze sewing needles, agricultural terraces, and a ceramic drum—bothered me for years to come. But as I discovered more about the Mexica Empire and its people—through further excavations and historical research—I came to a new understanding of what life was like for the people of ancient Capilco, Cuexcomate, and other sites in this imperial province. My excavations showed that even the most remote Aztec village had marketplaces visited by professional merchants who brought rare foreign goods such as bronze needles and bells. How could Aztec peasants afford bronze needles, crystal jewelry, and other valuable imports? The residents of these communities were skilled farmers who built terraced fields where they reaped rich harvests of grain, cotton, and other crops. Not only were they well off economically, but they also had a rich ceremonial life, full of music and dance. The ceramic drum was only the first indication; we later found fragments of flutes, whistles, and rattles. These provincial farmers had access to new styles and ideas from distant parts of the empire. More than this, these were resilient communities. They were able to withstand conquest by the Mexica Empire without giving up their traditional lifestyle and without becoming enslaved or impoverished by their new overlords. Their resilience, however, had a limit; the Spanish conquest of 1521 would destroy these communities.

That 1986 excavation season paved the way for a new understanding of life in Aztec society. For decades archaeologists had concentrated on Aztec pyramids and palaces, while historians gave their attention to kings, nobles, and ceremonies. This focus, which I call "monumental archaeology," still dominates the study of the early civilizations, from Mesopotamia and Egypt to the Inca and Aztec Empires. When commoners are mentioned at all, they are portrayed as downtrodden farmers who labored in their fields to produce food for the city people. Indeed, a common view of ancient civilizations—promoted by *National Geographic Magazine* and television documentaries—is that non-elite peoples were slaves toiling under the whip of a cruel overseer to build the pyramids and other monuments demanded by ancient despotic kings. But this is a highly inaccurate picture.

The bronze tools, musical instruments, and agricultural terraces we uncovered in 1986 no longer seem so mysterious or puzzling. For one thing, many more sites have been excavated in recent years. After my 1986 fieldwork at Capilco and Cuexcomate I followed up in the 1990s with more household excavations at an urban site, Yautepec. By the time my students started finding bronze tools, musical instruments, and agricultural terraces in my most recent excavations at the Aztec city of Calixtlahuaca in 2007, such finds no longer raised any eyebrows. At the same time, my colleagues and I have improved our understanding of how ancient societies were organized. We now know that most ancient farmers and other common people were not downtrodden, poverty-stricken laborers, but instead the architects of prosperous and satisfying lives. They were able to do this not because ancient kings were benevolent and kind to their subjects, but rather because some communities of commoner households had the means to avoid or resist being exploited.

When these two developments—new fieldwork and conceptual advances—are applied to the Aztecs, the result is a very different picture of the society than when I started excavating in 1986. This book tells the story of Aztec provincial peoples and their lives. But to tell that story, I also need to tell another about my archaeological efforts to bring these common people to life after more than five centuries. And before that, I must try to dispel the old picture of Aztec society.

The Aztecs: bloodthirsty savages or just regular folks?

Of all ancient peoples, the Aztecs have one of the worst reputations (for general works on Aztec society and culture, see, Berdan 2005, 2014; Matos Moctezuma 1995; Rojas 2012; Smith 2012; Townsend 2009). When people hear the word Aztec, most think immediately of human sacrifice. The media promotes this image, with re-enactments of sacrificial ceremonies on television, in Hollywood movies about the bloody ceremonies of the Maya (cultural cousins of the Aztecs), and in magazine articles about the bloodthirsty Aztecs. Aztec religion has been sensationalized to the point where it is difficult to achieve a clear and objective picture. This faulty impression of the bloodthirsty Aztecs does have a historical origin, though.

Spanish conquistadors exaggerated the extent of Aztec human sacrifice in order to justify their actions. Cortés and his soldiers killed thousands of Aztecs in warfare, and the diseases they brought—smallpox, hemorrhagic fever, and others—killed millions more. The Aztec peoples were then enslaved and forced to work in mines and on plantations. Their culture was destroyed. The Spaniards justified their actions by claiming the Aztecs were savages who engaged in human sacrifice on a grand scale. This activity had to be stopped, they argued, and the people converted to Christianity. Writers today who accept the words of the conquistadors at face value tell us that the Aztecs sacrificed many thousands of victims each year. At the other extreme, some writers today claim the Spaniards made up the whole idea of Aztec human sacrifice. The Aztecs, they say, had a peaceful religion that did not include the ritualized killing of people. Modern scholars (such as me) are sometimes accused by these writers of accepting the lies of the conquistadors and promoting the bloody Aztecs stereotype.

So where does the truth lie? Archaeological excavation proves beyond a doubt that the Aztecs did indeed practice human sacrifice. Although I have not excavated any sacrificial burials in my own projects, my colleagues who work on temples and ceremonial deposits have uncovered countless examples of human bones and offerings from sacrificial rituals. For example, a chamber under the floor of a small shrine at the site of Teopanzolco (in Cuernavaca) contained ninety-two human skulls, one-third of which were found together with the upper neck bones, a sure signal of decapitation (Smith 2008: 35). The sacrifice-deniers are wrong, and the conquistadors were right—at least about the existence of human sacrifice. Current evidence, unfortunately, does not indicate clearly the extent of human sacrifice in Aztec society. Did they sacrifice ten victims a year, 100, or 1,000? We simply cannot say (Dodds Pennock 2008; Smith 2012: 219–225).

Regardless of the precise number of sacrifices carried out at Aztec temples, the fact remains that this bloody and violent act was part of Aztec religion and society. But should this one practice color our whole view of these people? Most writers who want to counter the over-emphasis on sacrifice, blood, and violence point to art and poetry. Aztec artists created many exquisite works of art, particularly stone sculptures, gold jewelry, and beautiful and unique works of feather art (Figure 1.2). Aztec poets wrote poignant lyrical verse. Poetry was called "flowery speech," and this verse is an ode to a poet:

FIGURE 1.2 Aztec gold pendants, made with the lost-wax method. © Dumbarton Oaks, Pre-Columbian Collection, Washington, DC. Reproduced with permission.

> The flowers sprout, they are fresh, they grow;
> they open their blossoms,
> and from within emerge the flowers of song;
> among men You scatter them, You send them.
> You are the singer!
>
> *(León-Portilla 1963: 77)*

The Aztecs had a complex, multifaceted culture, some of which appeals to us today while other parts repel us.

My own approach to correcting the sacrificial bias of popular accounts is to look at the lives of Aztec commoners. Their artifacts show that people participated in a variety of rituals and ceremonies, but not human sacrifice, which was a state-sponsored spectacle engineered by nobles and priests. The separation between the lives of commoners and the lives of the Aztec rich and famous—those nobles, kings, and priests—was deep. For now, I want to emphasize one aspect of the social class gulf in Aztec society and the way it influenced the nature of the available historical records.

With the exception of a few commoner bureaucrats and merchants, only members of the Aztec noble class were literate. Aztec writing could communicate only a very limited range of themes, primarily religion, taxes, and royal histories. Commoner life was simply not recorded. After the Spanish conquest, when Spanish friars and others compiled histories of the Aztecs, they interviewed nobles, not commoners, so the surviving historical records give us rich detail about the nobles and only a few tidbits about commoners.

Another bias in the available written sources comes from the expansion of the Mexica Empire. As they say, history is written by the winners. Most historical texts were written by and about the capital and its residents, not about those in the provinces. As a result of these biases, the standard historical accounts of the Aztecs are silent about commoner life outside the imperial capital. The main reason I started excavating Capilco, Cuexcomate, and other provincial sites was to address these imbalances in the written record by finding information on the lives of commoners. My fieldwork results—and those of a few colleagues—now provide the first picture of the everyday lives of people in the provinces of the Mexica Empire. Their communities turn out to be more similar to communities today than I could have imagined.

The Aztecs were the last in a long line of Mesoamerican cultures stretching back more than two millennia. Aztec commoners were the people who carried ancient Mesoamerican cultural traditions into the Spanish colonial period, and their descendants transmitted this tradition through the subsequent centuries. When we order tacos and beans at a Mexican restaurant today, we can thank Aztec peasants more than their noble overlords. The basic elements of Mesoamerican cuisine (and many other traits, from language to myth to house construction) have been preserved across the Spanish conquest only because the peasants continued their traditional lives and practices. Their noble overlords, in contrast, did everything they could to act like Spaniards, from eating wheat bread to speaking Spanish to riding horses. Aztec farmers and other commoners are the unsung heroes of their culture, the ones responsible for carrying it into the Spanish colonial period and on up to the present.

Who were the Aztecs, anyway?

Many aspects of Aztec culture and society originated with earlier Mesoamerican groups such as the Maya, the Toltecs, and the people of the ancient city of Teotihuacan. The Aztec story itself begins around AD 1100, when a series of migrant groups arrived in central Mexico. They spoke the Nahuatl language and claimed to have come from Aztlan, a mythical homeland located somewhere to the north. No one has managed to locate Aztlan, and this leads me to believe that the term did not refer to a specific town or place. The new immigrants arrived just as the older Toltec civilization was crumbling. Leaders of the migrating groups declared themselves kings and built towns with palaces and temples. While these claims of kingship were apparently accepted by the people, the rulers did not have much power. Each king ruled a city-state: a few thousand people living in a small capital and the surrounding countryside.

For two centuries, the city-states grew in size while their petty kings competed with one another for dominance. I call this time, from AD 1100 to 1300, the *Settlement Period*.[1] It was a time of migration and the establishment of new cities, towns, and villages throughout central Mexico. Two of the sites I excavated—Yautepec and Capilco—were founded by immigrants from Aztlan early in the Settlement Period. This was followed by the *Growth Period* from 1300 until around 1430, when the population grew rapidly and many new settlements were founded, including one of my sites—Cuexcomate—and the Mexica capital Tenochtitlan.

A small empire (the Tepanec Empire) ruled much of central Mexico from the 1370s until 1428, when it was defeated by a coalition of city-states. Three of the victors—Tenochtitlan, Texcoco, and Tlacopan—formed an alliance and began a program of military expansion that would take them to the Atlantic and Pacific Oceans. I call this period, from 1430 until 1520, the *Imperial Period*. This "Triple Alliance" is today called either the Aztec Empire or the Mexica Empire. Although the term "empire" sounds very authoritative and powerful, in fact the Mexica Empire was really nothing but a big mafia-like protection racket. The Mexica were the people of Tenochtitlan, and the Mexica kings were the rulers of the empire. I use the term "Aztec" to refer to all of the peoples of central Mexico in the final four centuries before the arrival of Cortés. The sites I excavated were located in what is now the Mexican state of Morelos, and the people who lived at these sites called themselves the Tlahuica, one of many local ethnic groups within Aztec society.

Aztec families and households

During my fieldwork, first at Capilco and Cuexcomate and later at Yautepec, I was struck with the abundance of goods at every house. Each trash heap had numerous imported items and a diversity of ritual objects—from musical instruments to incense burners—that signaled a rich ceremonial life. There was enough food, and diets were more than adequate. Indeed, the most basic finding of my excavations is that these were successful households and communities. They grew and flourished for four centuries. Their members were prosperous and creative in forging an enduring way of life. Before my excavations, scholars knew next to nothing about Aztec households and communities, much less their success or failure. Why? Because no one had excavated enough Aztec houses to reconstruct the conditions of communities or families. But the answer also involves the development of new concepts. I was lucky that my fieldwork coincided with a fresh approach to understanding past societies called household analysis.

In the 1970s and 1980s, anthropologists and historians working in many parts of the world came to recognize the importance of studying the common people in society. The topic of "household studies" became a major focus of research. Scholars developed new concepts and methods to better understand commoners and their ways of life. Archaeologists picked up on this new approach and quickly realized that by excavating ancient houses and households—instead of tombs and palaces—they could for the first time look directly at the lives of past peoples who were not kings or nobles. Archaeologists could now figure out what people ate, the kinds of things they did in their homes, how they made a living, and their social and economic situation.

This new perspective, called "household archaeology," rapidly developed into an alternative to the traditional methods of "monumental archaeology." One of the founding works of household archaeology was a 1976 book titled, *The Early Mesoamerican Village*, edited by Kent Flannery, a creative and innovative archaeologist at the University of Michigan. I read this book as a graduate student and got excited about household archaeology. Just the names of the chapters stirred my imagination: "Analyzing Household Activities," or "Obsidian Exchange in Formative Mesoamerica." Even, "Relative Efficiencies of Sampling Techniques for Archaeological Surveys" (I'm serious here).

I wanted to discover and map house walls and storage pits; I wanted to find the trash heaps that would reveal what people were doing in their homes; and I wanted to use domestic remains to reconstruct life and society in the Aztec past. Excavating houses was what I wanted to do for my career. As soon as I had my Ph.D. degree I began excavating the Aztec provincial houses described in this book. The three chapter titles from Flannery's book listed above all describe topics I would eventually study at these sites.

In the field of household studies, the household—not the family—is the target of research (Carballo 2011; Flannery 1976; Netting 1993; Netting et al. 1984; Wilk and Ashmore 1988). A family is a group of close relatives, whereas a household is a collection of people who live together under one roof. Households often correspond to families, but they frequently include non-kin living in the same house. The family–household distinction is important because in many parts of the world (including Aztec Mexico) servants or lodgers play important roles in the activities of the household. In rural areas, where life centers on farming, the ability to have non-kin join and participate in household activities creates flexibility, and flexibility is one of the keys to the success of the Morelos communities. The household concept is particularly important for archaeology. While archaeologists can rarely work out kinship relations of ancient families, we can easily study activities and conditions of individual households—that is, of the group of people who lived and worked together in a single house. It is always important to keep track of the difference between the two key concepts of household archaeology: the house (as the building where people once lived) and the household (the people who lived there).

The people who once lived in the houses I excavated had devised prosperous ways of life. In modern terms, they had a high quality of life. This notion includes two parts: wealth and the ability to achieve a good life. The first is a more straightforward concept, one that is not too difficult to measure with archaeological data. Although the ability to achieve a good life might sound like a difficult topic for archaeology, the work of Nobel Prize-winning economist Amartya Sen provides an opening. To Sen, household or individual prosperity is not just about having resources, but it also involves the ability of individuals to exercise their human "capabilities" to achieve the goals they value. Many writers on economic development follow Sen's capabilities approach, which has been incorporated into measures such as the "Human Development Index" used by the United Nations, including Phillips (2006) and Sen (1992); I will apply this concept to my sites in Chapter 4 below.

Aztec communities

One reason for the success of the Aztec peasants lay in the nature of their communities. A community is a group of people who interact with one another and share some kind of bond. Today many communities are not limited to a single location; members of online communities may be scattered all over the globe. Nevertheless, the local community or neighborhood remains a crucial social group today, just as it was in traditional societies such as Aztec central Mexico. As I reconstructed the ancient communities of Capilco, Cuexcomate, and Yautepec, I was struck by their similarities with my own neighborhood and other communities today (Figure 1.3).

One reason communities are important is that their members can act together to achieve results not possible for individual families or households. But the value of communities goes farther than this. Economists Samuel Bowles and Herbert Gintis describe how modern communities often surpass governments and markets in providing services, caring for members, and upholding social norms. Elinor Ostrom won the Nobel Prize in Economics in 2009 for showing the success of traditional rural communities in managing what is known as common-pool resources (forests and fisheries). These communities use (and conserve) resources in ways that are more profitable and more sustainable then either government regulation or free-market transactions (Bowles and Gintis 2002; Ostrom 1990); see Chapter 7 below.

FIGURE 1.3 The village of Capilco. Drawing by Kagan McLeod.

Successful and prosperous groups and societies last for a long time. Many writers on sustainable communities today emphasize the importance of continuity and stability through time. The Congress for the New Urbanism is a group of planners and architects who work to create more livable, sustainable, and positive communities today. They keep a list of positive principles for urban planning, and it includes "long life and permanence, rather than transience" (Congress for the New Urbanism 2008: 2; Dempsey et al. 2011). The basis for community longevity, according to economists Bowles and Gintis, "is to be sought not in the survival of vestigial values of an earlier age, but in the capacity of communities, like that of markets and states, to provide successful solutions for solving contemporary problems of social coordination" (Bowles and Gintis 2002: F433). In other words, members of a community can work together to solve problems and accomplish common goals, and this leads to longevity and continuity.

One reason why economists, sociologists, and urban planners are concerned to describe and promote successful communities today is a general sense that the social bonds within communities are declining in modern society. The very title of Robert Putnam's (2000) book on this situation—*Bowling Alone: The Collapse and Revival of Community in America*—is an evocative comment on the growing individualism of modern society. A few decades ago bowling leagues were popular and gave people a setting where they interacted with their neighbors to create a sense of community. Now most people bowl alone as individuals, not as members of teams or leagues. The new field of "happiness studies" reports that levels of satisfaction and happiness are declining in the developed world. Writers on sustainability such as Bill McKibben decry the replacement of community cohesion with what he calls hyper-individualism. His solution is a return to local economies and to practices of people working together with their neighbors (Layard 2006; McKibben 2007; Putnam 2000).

Can Aztec sites provide any insights to help us understand communities today? I believe they can, and that is one reason I wrote this book. One of archaeology's big claims to fame is our ability to study human groups and behavior over the long term. But I have to admit that I wasn't thinking about communities and prosperity when I started excavating Aztec peasant houses in 1986. The relevance of my excavations for understanding communities over time only became clear over the years as I excavated several sites and thought about the results.

My journey to Aztec households and communities

My purpose in writing this book is to tell the story of a remarkable group of households and communities whose remains and trash were preserved at three archaeological sites in the state of Morelos, Mexico. To tell that story, I need to describe the ways I excavated these houses and how I analyzed their artifacts. I have four goals. First, I'll show how modern archaeology can reconstruct the lives and activities of the common people of the past. This is a departure from the common archaeological obsession with temples, palaces, and monuments. It also diverges from the kind of archaeology often in the news—finds of the earliest or the largest this or that from the past. The key to the new household archaeology is the excavation of houses and the study of their inhabitants from the trash heap. Piles of garbage behind the houses—called middens by archaeologists—contain the broken objects that allow archaeologists to reconstruct the lives and social conditions of ancient households.

Archaeological fieldwork does not take place in a vacuum; it is a human affair with all the messiness, joy, and sorrow of any human undertaking. The story of my excavations is also the story of a long episode of my family life. My second goal is to show how fieldwork and family came together over fifteen years and seven trips to Mexico. Cindy and I lived and raised our daughters—April and Heather—in the state capital, Cuernavaca, while excavating Aztec houses and analyzing artifacts from the ancient trash thrown out by their residents. These experiences had a profound impact on April and Heather (and on Cindy and me), and part of this book is their story as well as mine.

My third goal is to explain how and why the people whose houses I excavated forged a successful way of life, one that was resilient to outside conquest by the Mexica Empire and sustainable for many centuries. But success and sustainability have their limits, and in this case those limits came into sharp focus when Hernan Cortés conquered the Mexica Empire in 1521. Soon after, two of these communities were in ruins and the third was transformed radically.

My fourth goal in writing this book is to humanize the Aztecs. It is impossible to deny that Aztec priests carried out bloody rituals of human sacrifice on top of tall pyramids. But away from the central temples Aztec life was quite ordinary.

Aztec commoners—95 percent of the population—resembled their counterparts in the other ancient civilizations around the world, from Egypt to Peru. When I describe the remains of everyday activities—cooking tortillas, eating dinner, mending clothing, attending the market—a picture emerges of ordinary people making a living and creating a successful way of life. Practices like human sacrifice, carried out by priests and kings, formed little or no part of everyday life.

Note

1 These time periods line up with the technical labels used by archaeologists as follows. The Settlement Period corresponds to the Middle Postclassic Period in Mesoamerica and the Early Aztec Period in the Valley of Mexico. The Growth and Imperial Periods together comprise the Late Postclassic Period in Mesoamerica, also known as the Late Aztec Period in the Valley of Mexico.

2

THE DISCOVERY OF AZTEC PEASANTS

"What is the most exciting find you have ever made?" Archaeologists get this question all the time. People want to hear something like the opening of an ancient tomb, or uncovering the earliest Aztec temple, or finding Montezuma's gold treasure. These are the kinds of discoveries one sees on television programs or in the pages of *National Geographic Magazine*. At first, I used to deflect the conversation to other matters. This isn't the kind of archaeology I do. I don't uncover flashy finds. Although going after treasure in the manner of Indiana Jones is not what archaeology is all about, finding tombs and palaces is still a major activity for many archaeologists. Perhaps if I worked on the ancient mammoth hunters of Siberia my preoccupation with mundane and fragmentary artifacts might make sense. But since I excavate Aztec sites, people assume I must be looking for gold or sacrificial burials.

After I got tired of deflecting the "most exciting find" question, I decided to embrace it. My standard answer now is that my most important finds are bronze sewing needles. No, I hadn't found the earliest bronze needles, and I didn't discover the smelting technology for the first time. Rather, I had excavated these tools in the trash heaps out behind the houses of Aztec peasants. Not very thrilling stuff in comparison with a new tomb or pyramid, but if we want to learn about the Aztec people, these needles are really quite exciting.

The very fact that the poorest Aztec farming families had bronze needles in their domestic toolkits reveals more about their way of life than finding ten new temples. The needles (along with spindle whorls and other artifacts) tell us that the women of these houses were spinning, weaving, and sewing cotton cloth. Cloth was not only used for clothing, but it was also one of the forms of money in the Aztec economy. Back then, manufacturing money at home was not a crime. Needles and other items of bronze also tell us that these farmers were able to purchase goods imported from hundreds of miles away, where the bronze was smelted. Our needles and bells were the first batch of bronze items ever recovered from household contexts, and the first such artifacts that could be dated accurately.

Archaeologists who study daily life—and there are growing numbers of us—love ancient trash. The bronze needles at Capilco and Cuexcomate came from trash heaps next to houses. The technical term for these concentrations of old garbage is "midden." The Aztecs did not have municipal garbage pickup. People had fewer possessions and they threw away fewer items than we do today. They mostly just tossed their trash out back, where dogs and turkeys rooted around for the occasional tidbit. These heaps of trash built up over time, and after the sites were abandoned they were gradually buried as the soil built up. The organic materials rotted, leaving potsherds, stone tools, and bronze needles to sit in the ground until we came along to dig them up. These broken objects would provide the key to understanding the lives of Aztec farmers.

The story of my excavation—how I found the sites, how we excavated them, and how I figured out what it all means—may not meet the cinematic standards of Indiana Jones, but it's still pretty exciting. To start, what did I want to learn from these sites?

The invisible Aztec peasant

Before I started excavating, very little was known about Aztec peasants. The term "peasant" refers to rural farmers in agrarian states before industrialization—societies with rulers and governments, with cities and elites. Peasants differ from farmers in simpler tribal societies because they are subjects of lords and kings. They must produce enough food for the family as well as enough to pay their rent and taxes (obligations absent from tribal societies). Peasants were the backbone of ancient civilizations—they grew the food, fought in the armies, built the temples, and paid the rents and taxes. Does this mean peasants were exploited and impoverished? Or were they successful and independent? What were their lives like, and how did they respond to larger forces such as empires and markets? These were some of the questions that motivated my fieldwork.

Most of our knowledge of Aztec society comes from written documents. These tell us about everything from myths to armies to kings. What do the written sources say about Aztec peasants? Almost nothing. The best chronicler of Aztec society was the great Spanish friar Bernardino de Sahagún. He founded the first European school of higher learning in the Americas, the Imperial College of Santa Cruz Tlatelolco, in 1536 in Mexico City. With a team of young students (sons of the Aztec nobility) who were bilingual in Spanish and Nahuatl, Sahagún interviewed surviving nobles about life and religion before the arrival of Cortés. He then wrote up his findings in a twelve-volume book called the *Florentine Codex*. In this work, the single most informative description of Aztec life, here is what Sahagún said about Aztec farmers:

> The farmer . . . is bound to the soil; he works—works the soil, stirs the soil anew, prepares the soil; he weeds, breaks up the clods, hoes, levels the soil, makes furrows . . . he broadcasts seeds . . . provides holes for them . . . fills in the holes . . . gathers the maize, shucks the ears, removes the ears.
>
> *(Sahagún 1950–82: book 10: 41–42)*

Despite the stellar reputation of Friar Sahagún as the most insightful chronicler of Aztec society, his account of farmers is just not very informative. It is hardly surprising that farmers worked the soil, but how did they live? Were they prosperous or downtrodden? What was their role in society? The *Florentine Codex* contains a lot of detail about nobles and kings, about myths and rituals, and even about medicine and curing practices. But since Sahagún's informants—all nobles—did not know much about peasants, all we get are the boring generic remarks quoted above.

When Sahagún and other early Spanish writers do mention peasants, they are usually depicted as poor and powerless. They were the ones who paid the rent and taxes that supported nobles and kings. They were obligated to provide labor and serve in the military. They ran errands, they gathered firewood, and they seemed to live only to support the lifestyles of the Aztec rich and famous. The notion that Aztec peasants could have been prosperous, or that they might have had some level of control over their destiny, was completely foreign to the mindset of those who wrote the history of the Aztecs in the decades after the Spanish conquest.

This is where household archaeology finds its mission. Two types of archaeological finds overturned this bleak picture of Aztec peasants. First, I was able to uncover the foundations of the actual houses these people had built and lived in. Second, the ancient trash we excavated behind these houses paints a picture of how people were born, lived, and died. Much to my surprise, I found that these Aztec peasants were much wealthier and better-connected to the outside world than anyone had suspected. They also had more complex communities than Friar Sahagún—or the nobles who relied on them to live—would have guessed.

Background to the fieldwork

When the first shovel went into the ground at Capilco in early February 1986, it was a moment I had been eagerly anticipating for several years. I discovered archaeology as an undergraduate at Brandeis University. My advisor, archaeologist George Cowgill, helped arrange my first fieldwork experience in Mexico, where I participated in an archaeological survey project outside Mexico City. A friend and I lived in a rented room in San Juan Teotihuacan, a village built over the ancient ruins of Teotihuacan. We spent our days as part of a crew walking over the fields in the countryside north of Mexico City, looking for potsherds and other artifacts. Mounds were important—they were the ruins of buildings—and we had to make notes and take collections of artifacts from the ground. In my undergraduate enthusiasm I mistook a few ant hills for mounds. In my defense, some of those ant hills were quite large. One difference between them, I soon learned, was that when you stood on an ant hill to make notes, you ended up with lots of ant stings on your legs.

But I didn't mind the ant stings too much. I was thrilled to have the opportunity to be part of one of the final fieldwork projects of one of the most influential archaeologists working in Mexico, William T. Sanders. His enthusiasm for both fieldwork and the intellectual task of reconstructing the past was contagious, and I returned to the U.S. with a love of archaeology and a love of Mexico. I loved the countryside, the food, the music, and the people (but perhaps not the ants) to the extent that, after more than thirty years, I still go back to central Mexico almost every year for fieldwork and tacos.

Professor Cowgill was one of the directors of a long-term archaeological project at Teotihuacan, one of the largest and most important ancient cities in the Americas (Cowgill 2015; Millon et al. 1973). I wrote a senior honors thesis on the differences between the wealthy and poor residents of the site, based on the artifacts from their houses. This experience got me interested in urbanism and in the methods for interpreting ancient social patterns (such as the quality of life) from archaeological data. Although I claimed in my thesis that I could distinguish wealthy and poor lifestyles at Teotihuacan, the data were rough. It was difficult to tie the remains down to a single time period, and it was risky making grand social interpretations from a few hundred broken potsherds plowed up by modern farmers. I was frustrated and wondered if there wasn't a better method to study past societies archaeologically.

I went off to graduate school at the University of Illinois in the late 1970s, where I read Kent Flannery's 1976 book, *The Early Mesoamerican Village*, by flashlight in a tent. I immediately realized that the new household archaeology approach provided the answer to my frustrations. I wanted to dig some houses! I was working summers doing fieldwork and lab work under the direction of archaeologist Kenneth Hirth at the pre-Aztec urban center of Xochicalco, located in Morelos, not far from Cuernavaca (Figure 2.1). Hirth was planning to start digging houses at this hilltop city (Hirth 2000), and for my doctoral dissertation research project I was going to excavate houses at a rural site nearby to compare rural and urban households and study rural–urban differences.

Unfortunately, forces beyond my control intervened. I had two research grants lined up and I was ready to start, when the Mexican government made some changes in their system of granting excavation permits. At first it looked like I would only have to delay the start of my project by a year. So Cindy and I got married and spent our six-month honeymoon excavating at the Maya ruins of Copan in Honduras. Cindy was a fellow graduate student in archaeology at the University of Illinois in Urbana-Champaign. Her parents were both field biologists, and not surprisingly she brought a very scientific attitude to archaeology. Cindy had visited Cuernavaca in high school and loved the city, and I was coming to enjoy living there while working on the Xochicalco project. After our honeymoon amid the Mayan ruins, we spent the summer in Cuernavaca; I worked on Hirth's ceramics and refined my own fieldwork plans, and Cindy analyzed the animal bones from Xochicalco.

FIGURE 2.1 The ancient hilltop city of Xochicalco, showing my sites in the background. Photograph courtesy of Companía Mexicana de Aerofoto; reproduced with permission.

I soon found out, however, that as a student I could not apply for my own fieldwork permit. Furthermore, neither of the professional archaeologists I could work with (Ken Hirth and Jaime Litvak of Mexico's National University) would be able to help me for several years. So I changed my plans, and ended up working on ceramic classification and chronology at Aztec-period sites in Morelos. I first studied material I had helped excavate with Hirth at Xochicalco, and then I offered to analyze the ceramic artifacts from a series of excavations at Aztec sites by Mexican archaeologists. These archaeologists worked for the government archaeology institute, the Instituto Nacional de Antropología e Historia (INAH). Their job required a lot of fieldwork, but it did not give them enough time to analyze the resulting artifacts. An archaeological rule of thumb says that every month of excavation generates two to four months of artifact analysis. These scholars were more than happy to have me study their ceramics, and this work won me many brownie points within the Mexican archaeological establishment.

The downside was that the topic of my Ph.D. dissertation—ceramic classification and chronology—was not very sexy. Graduate students like to be on the cutting edge of research, with the latest methods and theories. While a study of household archaeology would have fit the bill, classification and chronology did not. But on the positive side, the research in my dissertation set the stage for all of my excavations over the next fifteen years, as described in this book. It turned out that my results could be applied to the new sites. The chronology (a sequence of time periods) was especially important: no archaeologist had previously succeeded in splitting apart the periods before and after the expansion of the Mexica Empire. Armed with this advance, I could examine, for the first time, the actual effects of Mexica conquest on provincial households. But first I had to find some houses to excavate.

Getting into the field

When I completed my Ph.D. in 1983, I looked around for sites where I could excavate houses and apply my chronology. During Hirth's fieldwork at Xochicalco, his crews scoured the landscape not only of the ancient city, but also of the surrounding mountainous countryside. Xochicalco sat at the edge of an area called the "Buenavista hills," a geological formation known as an alluvial fan. Alluvial fans have long, gently-sloping ridges separated by deep ravines. In this area the soils were thin and rocky and not very good for agriculture. Although Hirth's crew found a few suburban outliers of Xochicalco (AD 700–900), most of the nearby sites dated to the Aztec period (AD 1100–1521). These did not have much value to Hirth, who was looking for sites related to Xochicalco. But to me, these sites were perfect.

There are thousands of Aztec sites in central Mexico, mainly because of an ancient population explosion. But most are buried and it is hard to tell just where the houses are located. At two of Hirth's Aztec sites, however, the traces of houses were visible on the ground surface. They consisted of a very low mound, usually with the tops of one or two stone wall foundations visible at ground surface. The houses were very small, around twelve by fifteen feet. My first thought was that the small size indicated the poverty of their residents: poor peasants with few choices who had been forced out of areas with better soils into this rocky landscape. Centuries earlier Xochicalco had managed to thrive here, a powerful capital city whose territory probably included much good farmland at some distance. In contrast, the Aztec sites were small peasant villages whose residents had only the land nearby to make a living. My next task was to get funding and permission to excavate.

Beyond good sites for excavating houses, the state of Morelos held other attractions. Cindy and I both loved the city of Cuernavaca, capital of Morelos. Our first daughter, April, was born while I was still in graduate school, writing my dissertation. Our second daughter, Heather, was born soon after I started my first teaching position, at Loyola University of Chicago. We had heard horror stories of the young children of archaeologists getting very sick or injured in remote locations, a day's drive from the nearest country doctor. We could live in Cuernavaca, a large city with excellent medical facilities and good schools, and feel that our children would be protected. The fact that Cuernavaca was an attractive colonial city with beautiful weather didn't hurt. This city, whose motto is "the city of eternal springtime," became our second home for the next fifteen years.

The next step was to obtain funding. Archaeologists who work on spectacular temples and tombs, particularly at Greek, Roman, and Egyptian sites, seem to find wealthy private donors to finance their fieldwork. Some of my colleagues who excavate temples in the Maya region have private backing. These archaeologists tend to be very closed-mouth about their financial backers; they aren't anxious to share funding sources with their colleagues. In spite of some half-hearted attempts, I haven't yet located a wealthy patron interested in Aztec peasant houses. This means I have to submit detailed grant proposals to government agencies and private funding institutions. I succeeded in getting funding from the National Science Foundation. This required describing the sites and how I planned to use rigorous methods to achieve scientifically reliable results. As a small university trying to improve its research ranking, Loyola University was very helpful in obtaining grants and supporting my fieldwork.

With funding in hand, the final task was to get permission from the Mexican government. All archaeological projects, both national and foreign, have to be approved by a central archaeology council of the national anthropology institute (INAH). Once I received my excavation permit, I began working with the local INAH office in Cuernavaca. The Director, archaeologist Norberto González, provided us with laboratory space and loaned us wheelbarrows, shovels, and other excavation equipment. This was the start of a long period of collaboration with Norberto and the other archaeologists and staff of the Cuernavaca INAH office.

The first job was to map the sites. After classes let out in May, 1985, Cindy, the girls, and I piled in the car for the 24-hour drive from Chicago to Cuernavaca. We rented a small house not far from the INAH center. I enlisted Jeffrey Price, a graduate student at the University of Georgia, to help with mapping. Jeff and I drove out to Xochicalco every day and lugged our mapping gear a few miles to Capilco and Cuexcomate. Cindy stayed in town with the girls (aged 1 and 4 at the time), whose education in Spanish language and Mexican culture began with neighborhood playmates. At the sites, Jeff and I used an old theodolite to produce hand-drawn maps of Cuexcomate and Capilco. It took us six weeks to map twenty houses at Capilco and 150 houses at Cuexcomate. Our maps confirmed my initial impression that these sites consisted of very small houses, although we did map a much larger complex of mounds at Cuexcomate (Group 6) that turned out to be the remains of a noble's residence. We also located some check-dams, a type of agricultural terrace that would later help answer the question of how the residents of these sites not only survived but actually flourished in this marginal agricultural zone.

We then piled back into the car for the return trip to Chicago. Over the years we made no fewer than seven car trips from our home in the U.S. to Cuernavaca, always with both girls. Sometimes we drove two vehicles (a car and a pickup truck), and stayed in contact with walkie-talkies. Looking back, those first trips were probably the easiest ones. It took several days of driving, and once we figured out which gas stations had clean bathrooms (not always easy to find along Mexican highways), and which restaurants good food (an easier task), our drives got into a routine and we all looked forward to the stops along the way. While Cindy and I had thought that as the girls got older they would become better car travelers, in fact they learned how to torment one another, how to push each other's buttons, more effectively. We played car games (spotting license plates from U.S. and Mexican states), sang songs, and gave the girls books and toys for the car.

After a few months in Mexico, we were always hungry for a big salad when we crossed back into Texas. Lettuce in Mexico is notorious for possible contamination and it is best to avoid it. Today the situation is much better and these days I actually order salads in some restaurants, almost unheard of in the 1980s. After stopping at Pizza Hut in Laredo, Texas, for a salad and pizza on that first trip home, Cindy noticed toddler Heather chewing gum.

"Did you give her gum?" she asked me.

"Nope, I thought you did. Heather, where did you get the gum?"

"At the restaurant. Under the table."

Back at Loyola University in Chicago, I taught for the fall semester. In central Mexico, rainfall varies with the seasons. The dry season runs from January through May, with little rain. Then for several months it rains five or six days a week. The best time for fieldwork is during the dry season; January is also an excellent time to leave windy and cold Chicago for the eternal springtime of Cuernavaca. In January, we assembled a group of graduate students and drove two vehicles to Mexico. One student had planned to bring his old pickup truck, but it died that fall. My father, Dudley B. Smith, had recently retired and moved from New York to the Oregon coast. He came to the rescue by donating his pickup truck to the cause. (He did this partly to help us out, and partly to justify to my mother his need for a new truck.) Grants never cover all the costs of fieldwork, and Dad's truck was a very welcome (and sturdy) addition to the project.

Digging houses at Capilco[1]

That trip to Mexico was one of the most difficult. After loading up our field gear in a rented trailer, April and I flew to California to get Dad's truck, which we drove to San Antonio, Texas. There, we met up with Cindy, who arrived with a car full of students (and Heather) and the trailer of gear. In San Antonio we transferred the gear to the truck and headed south with both vehicles. As we approached Mexico City, I made the (bad) decision to bypass the city by driving west to Toluca and then directly, through the mountains, to Cuernavaca. The road to Toluca turned out to be in much worse condition than we anticipated, making progress slow. Heather got very ill and could not stop vomiting. We got lost in Toluca, the sun set, and it started raining hard. The walkie-talkies didn't work. We knew the road to Cuernavaca was treacherous, so we decided to head into Mexico City and find a doctor.

During the very tense drive to Mexico City, at night in a driving rainstorm, Heather's situation was getting grave. She was becoming dehydrated and listless. We asked people on the street for directions to a hospital, and lost a lot of time driving around in the dark. We finally realized that we were not going to find a hospital that way, and Cindy and I decided to head for one place we knew how to find—the Hotel María Cristina. The hotel's physician examined Heather and prescribed an antibiotic and electrolyte fluid. After a night of rest Heather began to improve and we headed for Cuernavaca. Much of Mexico City was a scene of destruction. A powerful earthquake had hit the city a few months earlier, and many buildings had collapsed. As we drove down the famous Insurgentes Boulevard, we could see that the rubble had only been partially cleaned up. All in all, that was the scariest and most difficult of all our drives to Mexico.

Once we arrived in Cuernavaca, it took a few days to get our field gear in order and assemble a crew of local workers. We hired local farmers—*campesinos* or peasants—to do much of the actual digging. The dry season is their off-season, and they are glad for the work. Most of the workers lived in the closest village, Tetlama, located just north of the sites. These men understand soils far better than most U.S. students, an important skill for excavating. Jeff Price and I had mapped twenty houses at Capilco, and I now had to reconcile two different approaches to excavation: testing vs. complete excavation. Clearing entire houses is the most informative approach, but time-consuming. Digging smaller test-pits takes less time and would allow us to excavate more houses, but we would learn less about each one.

My solution was to combine the two approaches by testing ten houses and then digging two or three completely. Which ones should we pick? We studied our map of the site, and it was clear that Capilco was a small village. The remains consisted of twenty very low mounds with one or more stone walls visible on the ground. The houses all looked pretty much the same in their size and construction. The scientific way to pick cases to study is to use random sampling. If we choose the ten houses at random (using mathematically generated random numbers), we are justified in generalizing the results to the entire site. That is, we can infer that the sample of ten houses is representative of all twenty structures. If we do not pick the houses randomly, then our results would be biased, pertaining only to the specific houses we excavate, not to the entire village of Capilco. The fact that houses were visible on the ground surface was a real luxury. Most Aztec sites are much more deeply buried and archaeologists have no idea how many houses they contain, or where the houses are located. When I later moved to Yautepec, such conditions would prevent the use of random sampling.

The first morning was spent clearing brush at Capilco. After lunch it was time to start digging, but I had forgotten to bring along a table of random numbers. So I improvised. I gathered twenty one-peso coins (these were large coins in 1986, the size of silver dollars) and labeled them with the numbers one to twenty. I borrowed a glass jar one of the workers had brought his lunch in, dropped in the coins and shook it up. The plan was to draw ten coins at random. I evidently shook the jar too vigorously, and before I could select any of the coins the jar broke, sending glass and coins flying in all directions. The students laughed, but our workers weren't sure how to react. As this was our first day, they were still uncertain about this strange group of foreigners. Did the boss just make a stupid mistake? Can we laugh? My incomprehensible act with coins in a jar probably confirmed their suspicions about odd gringo behavior. Undaunted, I picked up the coins, tossed them into my upturned straw hat, and blindly picked my random sample of ten house numbers. My scientific credentials intact with a random sample, we set to work.

The season started with four excavation teams. Each team consisted of an archaeologist crew chief and four to eight workers. Two of the archaeologists were U.S. graduate students, one was a Mexican student, and Cindy was the fourth. We enrolled our daughters in preschool in Cuernavaca. They had a great time, and before long were speaking Spanish better than Cindy or me. Our schedule for driving out to the site was organized around the girls' school day. We drove two vehicles out from Cuernavaca every day, and either Cindy or I would have to leave the excavations early in the afternoon to pick up April and Heather.

Work on a house began by having the workers clear the grass and low vegetation around the structure (Figure 2.2). Then the crew chief used strings and stakes to lay out a square grid, following the line of one of the visible house walls. The workers started excavating with small hand-picks and shovels. When someone found a feature such as a wall or floor, we switched to hand trowels. Delicate features such as human burials or offerings are cleared with paint brushes and dental picks.

We sieved all of the excavated dirt through a screen with 1/4-inch mesh (Figure 2.3). This helped us find small artifacts and standardize the size of the items saved. Every excavated level or context was given a catalog number, and the crew bagged up the various artifact types from each context separately. For each level we excavated, the archaeologist filled out a form, as well as forms for special samples such as charcoal for radiocarbon dating, or a soil sample for pollen extraction. The house walls had to be drawn in detail, with every rock carefully outlined, and any notable feature was drawn and photographed. The crew chiefs

FIGURE 2.2 Excavators starting to clear a house at Capilco. Photograph by Michael E. Smith.

FIGURE 2.3 Screening the excavated soil so that we don't miss the small artifacts. Photograph by Michael E. Smith.

would grumble about the time it took for all this record keeping, but such work is absolutely essential. Excavation is the systematic destruction of an archaeological site. Once the soils and features have been removed, it is impossible to go back and take another look, except through our notes and records.

For the ten houses in the random sample, the crew excavated one square (two by two meters) across a house wall to learn about the architecture and look for an interior floor or an exterior pavement. We also picked an exterior area for a second 2 × 2 meter trench to locate a midden. We used chemical testing to find areas with buried Aztec trash. When people live in an area over time, spilling food and dumping trash, a variety of biological waste products build up in the ground. Over the centuries, however, rainfall washes most of these substances out of the soil, leaving only the phosphates still in place. We used a rapid field test that shows the concentration of phosphate on a five-point scale. Scott O'Mack, our phosphate test specialist, took a series of soil samples on all sides of the houses. Where we found the highest reading, we placed our exterior test pit, and we almost always found a rich artifact deposit.

Bronze needles were not the only surprising artifacts to turn up in the Aztec trash deposits at Capilco. In fact, much of what we found in the middens did not square with the assumption that these people were impoverished and downtrodden. They had impressive access to foreign goods. Instead of using locally available stone or chert for their cutting tools, they imported obsidian—volcanic glass—from distant sources. A good deal of their everyday pottery was elaborately painted with geometric designs, and much of that was imported from a variety of areas within central Mexico, up to 100 miles distant. Besides bronze, people also got hold of jade beads and crystal jewelry made in even more distant places, as far as what is now Guatemala. They were well aware of fashions in the imperial capital and obtained the latest styles of ceramic figurines through trade. And the residents of Capilco had an active ceremonial life that included private rituals in households and public community celebrations. As we worked our way through the middens at Capilco, it dawned on me that my expectation for the residents of these sites—poor isolated peasants living their simple lives—was radically incorrect. Instead, these households were prosperous and successful. But the full documentation of the wealth, the connectedness, and the complexity of these farmers would not come until we had studied the artifacts in detail.

Fieldwork in rural Morelos presented a few challenges. We had to avoid the stinging ants that lived everywhere. You had to be careful when trying to sit in the shade of a tree, since the ground there was often covered with a vine whose leaves were coated with stinging hairs. This plant, called *mala mujer* ("bad woman"), produces a painful rash that can last for weeks. Our workers claimed that we needed to watch out for poisonous snakes that lurked everywhere. In fact, we only encountered a single snake—not poisonous—during six months of excavation. Its appearance at the site sure got our workers riled up, however, and excavation stopped for almost an hour while they chased it around (without success). The real danger was in the form of small scorpions with powerful stings. The standard advice for rural Mexico is that you shouldn't pick up a loose rock without first kicking it over to make sure it does not have a scorpion lurking on its lower side. After doing this for a few weeks and not seeing any scorpions, I decided not to bother kicking the rock that was going to serve to hammer a stake into the ground. So of course, as soon as I lifted it up, a scorpion crawled over to my hand. I dropped it quickly enough to avoid a sting. We kept an anti-scorpion antihistamine handy in our toolboxes, and had to use it a few times.

Meanwhile, after completing our sample of ten house tests, we picked two houses for complete excavation. The walls and floors of many houses had deteriorated over the centuries, so we chose houses whose architecture was in better shape, and whose artifacts pointed to occupation during all three of the time periods. In following out an exterior patio floor in one of these houses, we found it was attached to another structure, so we cleared that house too (Figure 2.4). All that was left were stone foundation walls, and sometimes a floor of smooth cobbles. The houses were all about the same size (about 15 feet by 15 feet), and their foundation walls were similar in construction.[2] But what kind of walls did these houses have above the stone foundations that we excavated? After digging a few additional houses at Cuexcomate we were able to figure this out.

FIGURE 2.4 Two excavated houses at Capilco. Photograph by Michael E. Smith.

More houses at Cuexcomate

We were finishing up at Capilco, and I went with the workers to cut some of the high, dense grass that covered the site of Cuexcomate. Some of the younger men wanted to burn the grass off, and asked me if they could get started. A couple of the older workers, however, thought a fire would be difficult to contain—it had not rained for a month, the grass was dry, and it was a windy day. I gave the order to avoid burning, and the men set to work with their machetes. Later on, I was some distance away photographing the check-dam terraces that bordered the site when a worker came running up to me, out of breath, and shouted, "You need to move your truck right away so that it doesn't catch fire!"

This was an odd suggestion. "Why would my truck catch fire?" I asked. Then it occurred to me—maybe they had started a fire after all.

"Well, a few guys did light a small grass fire to avoid using their machetes, and now it is out of control and moving toward your truck. You'd better hurry if you want to save it!"

I ran over to the truck and moved it a few hundred yards away from the line of advancing fire. The fire had got out of control, as predicted by the experienced workers, and was moving along with the wind. By now, it was impossible to simply stamp out the fire and I was getting worried. We cut a fire break (a strip without grass) and started a backfire to try to stop the flames, but the fire managed to jump over the break and keep going. I moved the truck again and we tried another fire break. I ended up moving my truck three or four times that morning while we fought the range fire. We finally extinguished the fire after it had burned half of Cuexcomate and a big area beyond the site.

No one was hurt, nor were the few skinny cattle who grazed in the area. The landowner hauled me into court looking for a payment, thinking (as many Mexicans do) that all gringos are rich. He had not suffered any economic damages, though, and I had twenty witnesses to my order not to light any fires that day. The landowner tried to figure out who started the fire, but the crew refused to say, and they deliberately kept that knowledge from me as well. The whole thing quickly blew over. But half of the site was now completely clear of grass! Later, I forgot to mention the fire to our ethnobotanist, who was looking for charred food remains (such as carbonized beans or maize kernels) in soil samples. She was puzzled about why the surface-level soil from half of the site was full of ashes and carbonized grass, while soil samples from the rest of the site had no traces at all of burning.

Spread out along a ridge between steep slopes, Cuexcomate is a much larger and more complicated site than Capilco (Figure 2.5). In addition to about 140 small rectangular houses just like those at the smaller site, Cuexcomate contains a formal open plaza bordered by mounds—ruins of structures built on platforms. Whereas Capilco was a village, Cuexcomate was a town. One of the mounds turned out to be a small temple, and across the plaza from it we tested a complex of mounds, Group 6, the residential compound of an elite household. The site also had a series of check-dam terraces in a ravine, and the slopes surrounding the site were covered with the remains of terrace walls. I designed a more complex scheme of random sampling to make sure that we: (1) picked structures in all parts of the site, and (2) included the platform structures as well as the more numerous small houses. This time I remembered to bring along my calculator with a random number generator. I picked twenty-one structures to test, and we got started. Although only a few

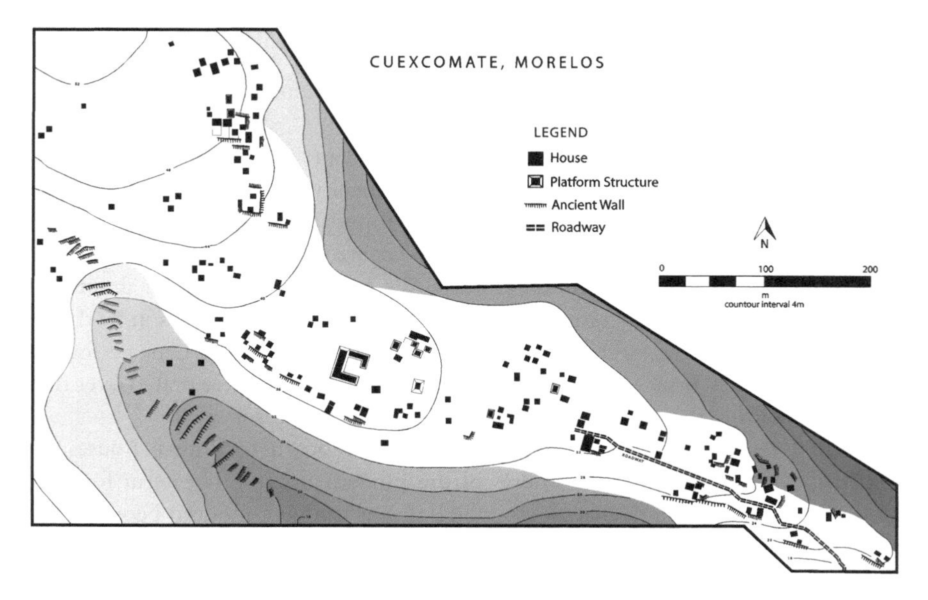

FIGURE 2.5 Map of Cuexcomate. Map by Michael E. Smith, drawing by Shelby Manney.

complete houses were cleared at Cuexcomate, we picked nine small houses, several platform structures, and some other contexts for partial excavations. But the question remained: what were the walls made of?

"Any idiot knows these walls were foundations for adobe bricks!"

Lunchtime conversation in the field typically switched back and forth between English and Spanish. One day I was discussing the problem of the house walls with the students. It was clear that the stone walls we excavated were foundation walls. There were simply not enough rocks around the houses for the walls to have been built of stone all the way to the roof (I actually had students count loose rocks around one set of houses to confirm this—not my most popular order). One possibility for the walls was sun-dried adobe bricks. Another was wattle-and-daub, a method in which a frame is made of dense rows of sticks ("wattle"), which is then filled in and covered with mud ("daub") that dries and hardens. Or perhaps the walls had been made entirely of wood.

While we were discussing this problem in Spanish over lunch, the oldest of our workers, Ángel Miranda, overheard the conversation. He remarked (in Spanish), "Any idiot knows these walls were foundations for adobe bricks!"

Ángel was the only one of our workers who could speak Nahuatl, and he was a great source of knowledge about traditional beliefs and practices. He would later become *compadre* to my wife and me when we sponsored his grandson's baptism; we became godparents (*padrinos*) to the baby, which made us compadres to the entire family. I replied to Ángel, "Okay, please tell us idiots how you know this."

"Because when we build an adobe brick house in Tetlama, we begin with stone foundation walls that look exactly like these walls we are excavating. Brick walls don't have this kind of foundation, and neither do other kinds of walls. Only adobe brick walls have this kind of stone foundation."

As I drove through Tetlama after work, I stopped and we all took a quick look at the foundation walls of a few adobe houses. Ángel was right—the Aztec walls we were excavating looked just like the modern foundation walls. Men in Tetlama build houses for their family. Many houses today are built of bricks and cement, but traditional adobe houses are still popular. We now had a hypothesis about the house walls, based on our comparison with modern traditional houses in Tetlama and other nearby villages. This hypothesis was later confirmed when we found fragments of adobe bricks in the excavations. Most bricks had deteriorated over the centuries, but due to accidents of preservation a few chunks survived.

Once I realized the ancient houses resembled modern traditional houses in Tetlama, we carried out some studies of the modern houses. The term for this kind of research is ethnoarchaeology, which means studying modern peoples and artifacts in order to gather information to interpret ancient peoples and artifacts. Ethnographers are anthropologists who study contemporary societies (whether rural or urban, whether in the developing world or the developed) by living with people and observing life as a participant. Unfortunately for archaeologists, ethnographers rarely bother to study the details of artifacts or houses. They might analyze family and kinship relations, but they will avoid things like house walls, granaries, or cookpots. Archaeologists realized some time ago that if we wanted this information, we needed to do our own ethnographic research on how modern peoples use objects, and this work is called ethnoarchaeology. This has become an important tool to help archaeologists come up with more detailed pictures of past societies.

One of our workers asked to take a few weeks off and then return. He had to build an adobe house for his father and wanted to finish before the rainy season started. He was worried that if he left the project we might not hire him back. I told him that if he would let some of the students observe him building the house and ask a bunch of annoying questions, I would keep him on the payroll. He thought this was an excellent deal—I paid him to build the house. In the process we got lots of information about how these adobe houses were built (Figure 2.6). The stone wall foundations were indeed identical to those we excavated. They were aligned and built with only strings and stakes, using mud for mortar. These were the same methods and materials the Aztecs used. We were only able to observe the first part of the construction process, though. It was getting toward the end of the excavation season and I could no longer afford to have students working on the modern house; we needed them to dig.

FIGURE 2.6 One of our workers building an adobe house in Tetlama. Photograph by Michael E. Smith.

The village of Tetlama

Our brief study of adobe house construction was one of many ways that Cindy and I, and our students, interacted with the people of Tetlama. Tetlama is a small village of several hundred farmers or campesinos. There are a couple of house-front shops and a small Catholic church, built in the 1500s. Our workers from Tetlama were a crucial ingredient of the success of the excavations. They were smart and hard working. Once we had trained them in our methods, they were able to do many of the mundane and complex tasks of fieldwork, from labeling bags to taking measurements of depth to excavating fragile remains like human burials. They were particularly good at identifying changes in the soil and carefully uncovering features such as burials. But the people of Tetlama also played an important role in our family life in Mexico.

Villagers hosted us for several fiestas, including a birthday party for Cindy, and we attended other events in town. Cindy and I became *compadres* with several families beyond the Mirandas. The way this works is that a couple—such as Cindy and I—are asked by another couple to sponsor one of their children. This can range anywhere from a serious life-long commitment—sponsorship of a baptism or a first confirmation in the church—to a minor social event, such as sponsorship of a child's graduation from sixth grade. Often more important than the bond between the child and his or her "Godparents" is the lasting formal relationship created between the couple and the parents. Instead of calling one another by name, the couples must address each other as *compadre* (for men), and *comadre* (for women). Sometimes there are specific financial obligations, but always there are more general obligations to support and help one's compadres. We once got a call late at night in Chicago asking for a "loan" to help a major compadre purchase a bull; we wired him the money the next day.

Many Tetlama families are too poor to fund a proper wedding, so they initiate compadre relationships to cover the major expenses. One couple will sponsor the cake, another will pay for the Mass, and someone else will hire the band. Cindy and I agreed to be the "compadres of the wedding dress" for the bride of one of Ángel Miranda's grandsons. Cindy went with the bride-to-be and her mother to pick out the dress in a Cuernavaca shop, and we paid for it and brought it out to Tetlama when the alterations were done. Our girls participated unofficially at the wedding; Heather, for example, helped hold the bride's train during part of the wedding procession through the village (Figure 2.7).

April and Heather spent considerable time in Tetlama. Cindy and I had obligations to see our compadres every time we came to the village, and each visit to the compadres required drinking some beers, eating a meal, and engaging in conversation. It might take an entire day to see all the compadres, and the girls used that time to run around and play with many new friends. They occasionally slept overnight in a dirt-floor adobe house, where they might be given the single family bed to sleep in. The girls learned skills that weren't taught in school back in the U.S.: how to feed the pigs, how to ride a mule, and how to grind corn and

FIGURE 2.7 Nine-year-old Heather participating in a wedding in Tetlama. Photograph by Cynthia Heath-Smith, reproduced with permission.

make tortillas by hand. They learned what life is like in a poor rural village. April and Heather came to recognize that as middle-class Americans they had opportunities—for education, for work, and for life—far beyond what their Tetlama friends would ever have. This first-hand lesson in rural poverty stuck with the girls, and to this day they have a greater understanding and appreciation for poverty and its effects than do most Americans.

April especially loved to play with the small chicks that ran everywhere in Tetlama. She would scoop them up and carry them around, cooing, "Mis pollitos! Mis pollitos!" (my little chicks). On every visit to the village she would ask if she could bring some of her pollitos back to the house in Cuernavaca. But we had no way to care for chickens, and our landlord owned two large German Shepherds that would not put up with chicks running around. Cindy and I had to check April's backpack and pockets to make sure all chicks stayed in Tetlama. Many years later, April married a farmer in upstate New York who does sustainable farming. She now has several pens full of chicks and chickens laying eggs. She told me, "I blame you and mom for my current obsession with chickens. If you had just let me keep some of those chicks from Tetlama, maybe I wouldn't be so fixated on chickens today." When she is working with the chicks on her farm, Cindy and I have heard her say affectionately, "Mis pollitos! Mis pollitos!"

The church where the wedding took place is a clue to the origins of the village of Tetlama. Shortly after the Spanish conquest a wave of forced resettlement swept through Mexico. Spanish colonial authorities did not want the natives living scattered across the landscape; they wanted people to live together in villages and towns where they could be counted, converted to Christianity, and put to work. New settlements were founded, each with a church, and the natives were forced to move into town. Capilco and Cuexcomate were emptied out, and those residents who had not died in one of the epidemics raging in Mexico moved into Tetlama.

Cindy and I still keep in touch with people in the village, and we value the lasting friendships we formed with a number of our workers and their families. I make sure to donate copies of our reports and books to the village, and to keep the people of Tetlama informed about our excavations at other sites. After all, they are the descendants of the original inhabitants of Capilco and Cuexcomate.

Where are all the bodies?

The Aztec period was a time of major population growth, and there were more people living in central Mexico than at any time before then. But what happened to all the bodies? Over the years my colleagues and I have found remarkably few burials at Aztec sites. Some archaeologists speculate that bodies were cremated and not buried. We do know from written sources that kings, merchants, and nobles were cremated, so perhaps commoners were, too. The problem with this explanation is that once a body was cremated, the ashes and fragments of burned bone were gathered up, placed in a ceramic urn, and buried. Only a few of these cremation urns have ever been excavated. I have a different explanation for the lack of bodies: people were buried in cemeteries that archaeologists simply have not managed to locate. Not a very satisfying explanation, I admit, but it is the only one that makes sense (Smith 2012).

Not everyone was buried in these hypothetical cemeteries, however. We excavated eight burials at Capilco and another three at Cuexcomate. All were infants and children. Most had been buried in a sitting position, under the house floor or in a simple pit grave next to the house. One was buried under a rock pile. The Aztecs believed that infants were gradually transformed into a full human being over their first few years, and perhaps this led to two different forms of burial: infants under and around the home, and older children and adults in cemeteries. The lack of formal tombs with rich offerings might be a signal that these infants had not achieved the status of full adults. Nevertheless, someone—most likely their parents—cared enough to dig a grave, carefully arrange the body in a sitting position, and arrange a few pots with the body as an offering. The placing of these burials under or next to the house was probably a symbolic act that acknowledged the closeness of kinship bonds and their anchoring in the family house. But we still did not find enough bodies. Infant mortality was undoubtedly high in Aztec villages, and if all of the children who died were buried in domestic locations, we would have found the remains of more than eleven individuals. This is one mystery I've never solved.

One day in the field, the buzzing of cicadas caused our workers to abandon the excavations and start scrambling up trees to catch these large insects. I blame my mother-in-law for this episode. Cindy's parents are both field biologists.

Her mother, Maxine Heath, is the world's expert on the classification of North American cicadas (Sanborn and Heath 2012), and her father, James Heath, studies temperature regulation in every type of animal, from polar bears to cicadas. Fieldwork for the Heaths consists of chasing down cicadas in the southwestern U.S. and taking measurements. Cindy and I—and April and Heather—have all participated in cicada-chasing. It's almost as much fun as excavating trash heaps.

Cindy's mother was interested in getting some specimens from Morelos. When we mentioned this to our workers, they offered to get us some good ones. Before long, the excavations were at a stand-still and the trees were full of guys trying to grab cicadas. We ended up with some nice specimens we brought back to the U.S., and no one managed to fall out of a tree.

Celebrating the end of the world

Contrary to popular opinion, the ancient Mayas did not predict the world would end in December, 2012. The Maya calendar did complete a major cycle and start a new one at that time, and the date was considered holy to the Mayas. But the notion that the renewal date marked the destruction of the world was invented by new-age writers in order to sell books. This idea is not found in the Maya chronicles. It is ironic that this bogus prophecy received so much publicity, while the fact that the Aztecs really did predict the end of the world has been ignored.

In Aztec mythology, the world has been created and destroyed by the gods four times previously. We are now in the fifth sun, or the fifth creation, and our age will end when the gods decide to cause earthquakes that will destroy the earth. The Aztec calendar completed a cycle and started over every fifty-two years (unlike the Maya calendar, whose cycles were thousands of years in length). The first day of the fifty-two-year cycle is the date chosen by the gods for destroying the world. Unfortunately, the Aztec prophecies did not say *which* cycle would be the deadly one. As a result, the Aztecs got worried every fifty-two years. They held a major celebration on New Year's Day at the start of each fifty-two-year cycle to give thanks to the gods for not destroying the world this time. This ceremony was an elaborate event called the "New Fire Ceremony." The last one before the arrival of Cortés was celebrated in the year 1507. What looked initially like simple piles of rocks at Cuexcomate turned out to be ceremonial dumps marking the New Fire Ceremony.

The Aztec year had eighteen months of twenty days, with an extra five days tacked on at the end to add up to 365 days, the length of the solar year. Those five days were considered the unluckiest days each year, and especially so in the fifty-second year of a cycle. According to Friar Sahagún, people threw out all of their household possessions and then started with new things if and when the next cycle began (my guess is that this ceremony was promoted by the potters, obsidian-knappers, and other crafters). On the final day all fires were extinguished and everyone waited around to see if life would continue into the next cycle. The head priests spent the night on top of a mountain near Tenochtitlan, watching the sky. When they saw the constellation of stars we call the Pleiades rise in the east, it was considered a signal from the gods that the world was spared and the sun would soon rise on a new period of fifty-two years. A human victim was sacrificed and the priests lit a new fire with a ceremonial fire drill. They carried a torch to light the sacred fire at the central temple in Tenochtitlan, and messengers lit torches from the sacred fire and carried them throughout the empire. It must have taken days for the fire to reach remote places like Capilco and Cuexcomate.

The rock piles at Cuexcomate are the most direct archaeological evidence anywhere for activities associated with the Aztec New Fire Ceremony. We excavated two rock piles completely and tested four others. At first I was puzzled by these features. Large rocks were concentrated in one place, but without an obvious shape. Underneath the stones were the remains of broken ceramic vessels, but these deposits differed from normal domestic middens in two ways: the sherds were more densely concentrated than in middens; and the sherds could be reassembled into whole and partial vessels. The potsherds in middens are normally fragmented and scattered, and we could never reassemble whole vessels. But we managed to glue together twelve pots just from the dump excavated by Osvaldo Sterpone, including the ceramic drum.

After some pondering, I realized that the artifact dumps looked like the results of people discarding their household goods in preparation for the New Fire Ceremony. A painting of this activity from the work of Friar Sahagún matches up nicely with what we found in the dumps under the rocks. A few years later, my colleague Christina Elson figured out that archaeologist George Vaillant had apparently excavated similar ritual dumps at the Aztec site of Chiconautla in the 1930s, but had not linked them to the New Fire Ceremony (Elson and Smith 2001).

Unfortunately, we cannot match up individual artifact dumps with specific New Fire celebrations. Cuexcomate was occupied from approximately 1350 until 1521, an interval that contained four New Fire ceremonies: 1351, 1403, 1455, and 1507. As an exercise in an undergraduate class on the Aztecs in 1975, we had to bring the Aztec calendar up to the present. Today this can be done by pushing a button on an internet site, but we had to do the calculations by hand. Much to our surprise we determined that a New Fire date occurred in the middle of the current semester! The class held an end-of-the-world party to celebrate, and then awoke the next morning with hangovers to find that the gods had granted humans another fifty-two years of existence. We are safe now until the year 2027, at which time the gods may or may not decide to destroy the world with earthquakes.

Farming the hillsides

Some writers assert that ancient peoples were completely preoccupied with death and the afterlife. Dynastic Egypt is the target of most of this nonsense, although the Aztecs and Mayas have not been immune. The New Fire Ceremony ritual dumps suggest that the residents of Cuexcomate did worry about the afterlife and the end of the world at least once every fifty-two years. But if these people were preoccupied with anything, it would have been their crops and the rains. They were peasants. If they couldn't farm effectively they would get in trouble with their landlord or the tax collector, and they might even starve. The grim reality of peasant life throughout the ages requires that the crops come first. In the Buenavista hills agricultural terracing provided the foundation on which people built successful households and communities.

Jeff Price and I had identified areas with check-dams next to both Capilco and Cuexcomate and mapped them in 1985. He returned in 1986 to supervise the excavation of several of them (Smith and Price 1994). These were the first Aztec check-dams to be excavated. Check-dams are stone walls built across a small ravine to trap soil and sediments carried in temporary streams after a good rainfall. Check-dams are still cultivated today by peasant farmers in some parts of Mexico, and we studied reports to get an idea of how our features may have functioned. The Otomi peoples have shared rural central Mexico with Nahuatl speakers from Aztec times to the present. In the mid-twentieth century, an Otomi-speaking farmer described check-dam farming as follows:

> A check-dam isn't built all at once. Usually a farmer starts with a low wall across the path of an *arroyo* (a small valley). It takes a few years until the water has brought down enough debris and soil to level with the top of the wall. Then, the farmer will build up the wall a bit more, and so on, little by little until he has built up a tall strong wall and a large level field. A well-made check-dam is level so that the trapped water will cover all parts of the field evenly . . . There is no need to fertilize a check-dam because every rainy season the water brings down new debris and soil.
>
> *(Wilken 1987: 101)*

The heavy seasonal rainstorms in central Mexico are ideal for check-dam farming. From our excavations and descriptions of modern check-dams we pieced together the way these features were built and used (Figure 2.8). Jeff's excavations behind the dams revealed many thin layers of soil, testimony to the annual flooding and sediment build-up. The check-dam fields can be quite large; as the soil builds up, the field moves up the arroyo walls and its surface area gets larger. The deposits contained pollen from some of the crops cultivated in the fields, and the chemical composition of the excavated sediments told us that ancient farmers had applied fertilizer to their fields.

Check-dams are highly productive agricultural fields. The soils are deep and rich, and during the rainy season they are well watered. Check-dams are a good example of what anthropologists call "intensive agriculture." They produce high yields, but at a cost: the farmer—and his household—must put in long hours to achieve those yields. Traditional farmers generally avoid intensive agriculture because they can grow crops more efficiently—that is, with less labor—by using other methods like rainfall farming without terraces or canals. Why then would farmers intensify their farming when it means more work? The answer is that sometimes difficult measures become worthwhile—even necessary—when there are too many people to support by non-intensive methods.

FIGURE 2.8 Men building a check-dam or terrace wall. Drawing by Kagan McLeod.

There was no need for terracing when the Buenavista hills were first settled by small groups at Capilco and other villages in the twelfth century. Rainfall farming could easily produce enough food. But over the centuries the population grew. New immigrants arrived and founded larger communities like Cuexcomate. Before long, people needed to adopt some form of intensive agriculture just to survive, and check-dams were one way to do this. Farmers had to work harder to get the higher yields of check-dam terraces. Compared to rainfall agriculture, the terrace farmer has to lug rocks to the field, set them in rows, and then monitor and repair the walls to keep them from washing away in a heavy downpour. When a noble and his extended household arrived at Cuexcomate around 1300, along with several hundred supporters and subjects, he somehow laid claim to the nearby land.

Beyond just feeding their families, farmers now had to pay rent to this new lord and pay taxes to the local city-state king.

Hillside terraces were a second form of intensive agriculture that expanded rapidly in the Buenavista hills. Farmers built low stone walls on sloping terrain, following the contour of the hill. Like check-dams, hillside terraces create productive fields on land that cannot be farmed with simple rainfall cultivation. Also like check-dams, they require constant maintenance in addition to the basic activities of soil preparation, planting, weeding, and harvesting involved in all farming.

The labor and technical know-how for both kinds of terrace fields came from individual households. The hillside terrace walls form a messy lattice of short segments without much geometric order. If one has seen the remains of Inca terraces in the Andes, the contrast is stark. Inca terraces are of uniform size and construction, and the nice parallel rows extend along the mountainside, often for miles. This geometric uniformity comes from centralized control. Inca terraces were built by large work gangs under the direction of state officials. The Morelos hillside terraces, on the other hand, were built by individual families; otherwise they would show greater precision and order. As for the check-dams, they require small bursts of labor at key times that are hard to predict (depending on the rainfall). There is no way a centralized work project could successfully build and maintain the check-dams I excavated; these too must have been built by individual households, acting on their own. Anthropologists call this kind of small-scale, household-level cultivation smallholder agriculture (Netting 1993).

The investment of labor in terraces is always greatest at their initial construction. But once built and functioning, the terraces at Capilco and Cuexcomate turned out to be a highly productive agricultural method well suited to both the environment and its residents. In fact, terracing by smallholder peasant farmers was one of the key developments that explains the resilience and success of these communities. One nagging doubt remained, however. Perhaps these terraces had been built and used in recent times rather than in the Aztec period. I asked Ángel Miranda and the other workers, and none of them had seen any such terrace farming in this region. Also, they had never heard their fathers or grandfathers talking about terraces. Later, when we were able to run some radiocarbon dates, they confirmed that the check-dams were indeed built and used before the Spanish conquest.

The rainy season begins and the excavation ends

The rainy season begins suddenly in Morelos. One week there is no rain, then a few downpours, and soon it is raining hard every day. We brought the excavations to a close just before the rains started. I then flew to Washington, DC, for a summer workshop on the Mexica Empire at the Dumbarton Oaks research center, leaving Cindy behind to supervise backfilling the excavations (and supervise our girls). The INAH authorities had decided that our modest peasant house foundations were not worthy of consolidation and preservation as ruins left open for the public.

We had excavated many more houses and features at Cuexcomate than originally planned. During winter and spring 1986, the Mexican economy was doing poorly and the value of the peso dropped continuously against the dollar. Loyola University wired me funds twice a month, and the same amount of dollars was converted to a larger number of pesos with each transfer. I used the additional funds to hire more workers and expand our excavations.

At one point excavations were open in so many parts of Cuexcomate that a herd of goats that passed through the site every day with an old goat-herder had trouble avoiding the trenches. The workers would joke with this guy about preparing barbecued goat—a local delicacy—should any of the animals disturb an excavation. None did, although we later learned that the herd owner was the father of several members of our Cuernavaca lab crew. We went to a fiesta at his house, and we were served barbecued goat from that very herd!

While I was in Washington, DC, Cindy and the crew backfilled the trenches with some help from the rains. What had we learned? In the monumental archaeology approach—digging temples and tombs and palaces—the major results are clear as soon as the finds are made in the field—discovery of a new royal tomb, the biggest palace, a hieroglyphic inscription, and the like. But when the goal is to learn about the mundane lives of commoners, it takes some time before we can grasp the results of the fieldwork. I had to analyze all of the potsherds and obsidian flakes—hundreds of thousands of fragments in total—before I would know much about these ancient peasants and their lives. So our student crew moved to the lab to write their reports and start classifying the artifacts.

Notes

1 The excavations at Capilco and Cuexcomate are described in detail in Smith (1992, 2015a).

2 I should explain why I did not employ some of the methods commonly used in other studies of household archaeology (Carballo 2011; Flannery 1976). At Capilco and Cuexcomate, the upper layers of soil had eroded away at some point between the abandonment of the houses and our excavations. This was good in that it left the wall foundations visible on the ground surface for mapping and study. But the erosion was bad in that it removed any evidence for the precise locations of activities in and around the houses. Because most of the excavated areas were garbage middens, it was not worthwhile to record the exact locations of artifacts (except for the very few offerings we found). The erosion also meant that it was not possible to identify ancient activity areas at the houses. When ancient deposits are better preserved, the piece-plotting of artifacts and reconstruction of activity areas are regular methods of household archaeology.

3

RECONSTRUCTING DAILY LIFE

The residents of Capilco and Cuexcomate managed to survive and even prosper in the marginal environment of the Buenavista hills. The terraces are the prominent landscape markers that show how they persevered, but it is the artifacts that furnish the details. Tools for spinning cotton thread, for example, signal prosperity because cotton cloth was a form of currency in the Aztec economy. The beans of the cacao or chocolate plant served as small change in Aztec markets, but large purchases were made with standard lengths of cotton cloth. People also paid their taxes with cloth money. The people of Capilco and Cuexcomate were literally manufacturing money in their homes, but this was not a crime as it would be today.

Aztec women throughout central Mexico spun and wove cotton cloth, but this activity was carried out at a much higher level at Capilco, Cuexcomate, Yautepec, and other places in Morelos. The reason is simple: Morelos is the only part of central Mexico where cotton can be grown. Cotton is a lowland crop that was cultivated most commonly in hot, rainy fields along the Gulf of Mexico. Within the central Mexican highlands, where most places have elevations of well over a mile, the state of Morelos is lower, with a warmer and rainier climate. People grew cotton in irrigated fields along the rivers of Morelos, and perhaps in check-dam fields throughout the Buenavista hills. Aztec households in other areas, in contrast, had to import their cotton, from either Morelos or the Gulf Coast.

How do we know textiles were produced at a higher level in Morelos than in other areas? How do we know they were made by women, and not men? How do we even know that people spun and wove at all in these houses? This important domestic activity provides a good illustration of how archaeologists work out the uses of artifacts. Potsherds and stone tools don't come out of the ground with labels saying "tortilla griddle" or "kitchen knife." The ways ancient people used such items must be determined through a process called reasoning by analogy.

Archaeologists frequently use analogies with modern traditional societies to figure out how artifacts were used in the past. For example, peasant households throughout Mesoamerica today use a large circular flat ceramic griddle called a *comal* to cook tortillas. We find thousands of sherds from flat ceramic clay vessels at Aztec sites, so we make an analogy with the uses of modern griddles and interpret the Aztec vessels as tortilla griddles.

Many tasks are involved in producing a piece of cotton cloth. You have to clean the cotton, spin fibers into thread, dye and prepare the thread, weave the cloth, and finish the item with sewing and embroidery. Two of these steps—spinning and sewing—involved the use of nonperishable tools that are preserved in middens. The most abundant are spindle whorls and spinning bowls of fired clay, and my interpretation of their use is based on an argument by analogy (Wylie 1985). First, I compare these items to modern spinning tools to establish a possible interpretation—a hypothesis—and then gather evidence to test the hypothesis. The artifacts in question are circular ceramic beads with a tiny hole in the center (called spindle whorls) and small bowls about three inches in diameter with little tripod supports (Figure 3.1). For the basic analogy or comparison, I focused on the way traditional Maya women spin cotton thread today. Women pull the fibers out by hand, twist them together and wind them around a long narrow wood spindle. A clay spindle whorl adds weight so that the spindle can twirl effectively, and the rotating spindle is controlled in a small bowl. Based on descriptions and observations of this process, archaeologists interpret the small beads and bowls as tools for spinning cotton.

FIGURE 3.1 Spindle whorls and spinning bowls for hand-spinning cotton. Photograph by Michael E. Smith.

Aztec sites typically contain two distinct sizes of spindle whorl—small and large—and we know from experimental studies that these were used to spin cotton and maguey thread, respectively. Maguey is a central Mexican agave plant whose fibers are good for making rope and coarse cloth similar to burlap. The sites I excavated are located in Morelos, where cotton was cultivated but not maguey (because of soil and weather conditions). The sites have lots of small whorls and spinning bowls but only a few large whorls, whereas sites in the Valley of Mexico (where maguey was grown but not cotton) have lots of large whorls and only a few small whorls or spinning bowls. The interpretation of the small beads as spindle whorls is a strong and obvious one. You simply cannot spin cotton by hand without these weights, and no one today doubts this functional interpretation. But the uses of the small bowls are not as obvious, since it is possible to spin cotton without them. A close look at these items, however, supports the textile interpretation. A few of our burials and offerings contained whole spinning bowls. The surface of the interior base of these small bowls is worn away. A twirling spindle would produce just this kind of wear pattern. Also, these bowls are highly standardized in their size, which suggests that they were manufactured to be the right size for a specific task.

All of this information—the wear patterns, the sizes of the objects, our knowledge of Aztec textiles, and the like—supports the hypothesis that the small artifacts were used for spinning cotton thread. But the strongest evidence is pictorial. The *Codex Mendoza* is a document painted by an Aztec scribe immediately after the Spanish conquest that illustrates, among other things, Aztec daily activities. It shows a mother teaching her seven-year-old daughter how to spin cotton thread, and a mother showing her fourteen-year old daughter how to weave. In the first image the spindle whorl and spinning bowl are clearly shown by the artist (Figure 3.2).[1]

Aztec textiles were made by women. Many documentary sources, from Friar Sahagún to the *Codex Mendoza* and others, state that not only did all women produce textiles—nobles and commoners alike—but this activity was an important part of their gender identity. Spinning and weaving were considered women's work, and women took pride in making cloth.

The logic of the argument outlined above—create an analogy and then test it with additional information—underlies most of my interpretations of excavated artifacts. It is the same kind of argument that let me use our ethnoarchaeological study of modern house construction to interpret the excavated houses. Another basic method I use is to count and weigh the artifacts. Most of my interpretations of domestic life and social conditions are based on quantification of artifacts, something that is given far greater emphasis in the methods of household archaeology compared to monumental archaeology. I will spare the gory details here; readers who want to see big tables of quantitative data can consult the technical articles and reports cited in the bibliography.

By Mexican law, all antiquities (artifacts, sites, features) belong to the Mexican nation, regardless of whether they are on public or private property. As national patrimony, the artifacts must be studied and stored in Mexico. Foreign archaeologists are permitted to export only small numbers of samples for technical analysis,

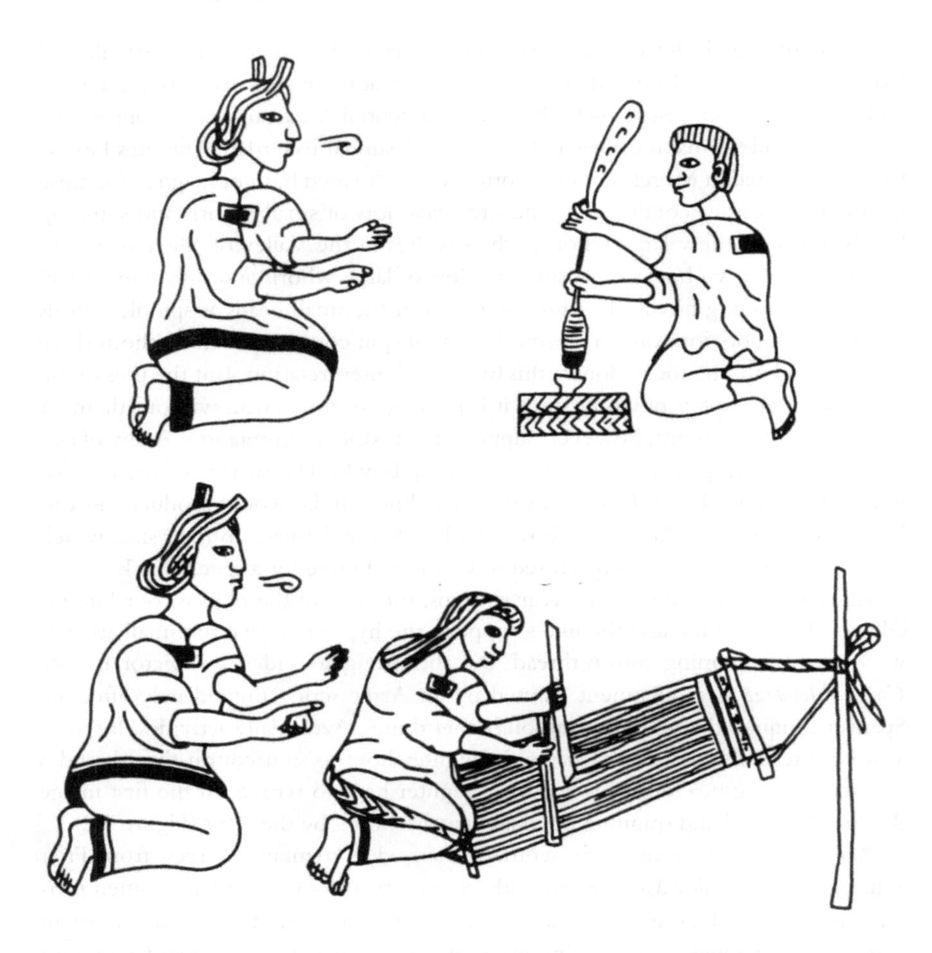

FIGURE 3.2 Mothers teaching their daughters. Top: a seven-year-old learns to spin cotton; bottom: a fourteen-year-old learns to weave cotton cloth. From the *Codex Mendoza* (Berdan and Anawalt 1992: folios 59r and 60r); reproduced courtesy of Frances F. Berdan.

but over 99 percent of the artifacts cannot leave the country. One implication is that Cindy, the girls, and I had to return to Cuernavaca every year to keep the lab work going. Given our love of Mexico, we all looked forward to the annual road trip to Cuernavaca.

Our lab in the Emperor Maximilian's stable[2]

Each day during the fieldwork we brought the newly excavated artifacts to our laboratory in Cuernavaca. This was part of the government (INAH) archaeology offices, a complex of historic buildings that originally served as a garrison for the soldiers of Maximilian I, the Austrian-born "Emperor of Mexico," from 1864 to 1867. Our lab was once the stable. Maximilian and his Empress Carlotta lived in the capital, Mexico City, but maintained a vacation retreat in Cuernavaca, just as many wealthy residents of Mexico City do today. In his Cuernavaca garrison Maximilian built a small house for his Indian mistress, who was known as the "India Bonita." Behind the INAH offices today is an ethnobotanical garden—that is, a botanical garden featuring plants that are useful to people. The garden is a lush and attractive forest of useful herbs, medicinal plants, and some ornamentals. Given the warm and rainy climate in Cuernavaca, this was a beautiful and verdant setting for an archaeological lab. The view out the window included the India Bonita's house, a formal pool, and the ethnobotanical garden in the background (Figure 3.3).

Our daily haul of artifacts typically included close to 100 bags containing many thousands of potsherds and other items. All of this had to be washed and cataloged. Cheryl Sutherland, my student at Loyola University, ran the lab. We hired a law student who had worked for INAH, Austreberto Encarnación, and asked him to find a crew of workers to wash the artifacts. We hired his fiancée, and then her sisters and brother, and eventually some of their friends. Our lab consisted of six large tables (plywood slabs on saw horses), with chairs, plus some storage shelves along the walls. Typically the tables were covered with hundreds or even thousands of potsherds being sorted into different types.

As our crew of local lab workers washed thousands of potsherds—a quarter million in total!—they became familiar with the different vessel forms and types

FIGURE 3.3 View from our lab window in Cuernavaca; the building on the right is the India Bonita's house. Photograph by Michael E. Smith.

of decoration. It was then an easy task to teach them to identify the ceramic types, and they were soon better at this than any of the archaeology students. At first this was puzzling. How did they learn so fast? Our experience with Mexican preschools supplied part of the answer. When April and Heather started preschool in Cuernavaca, we were intrigued by an activity called *manualidades*. One translation of this term is "manual arts or crafts," but that does not capture its meaning very well. Kids in Mexican preschools and elementary grades spend considerable time manipulating and classifying small objects. Heather remembers sorting buttons into piles by their size and color. Kids move small pieces around and manipulate them in various ways. They draw small objects over and over, from squares and triangles to boxes and towers. While children in U.S. schools also do some of these things, the physical manipulation of small objects is given much more emphasis in Mexican schools. Kids spend more time on *manualidades* in Mexico, and there are more variations in what they do.

My theory is that early training in *manualidades* is the edge that gives the average Mexican a much better grasp on classifying artifacts than the average American. Very few untrained U.S. students have learned our ceramic typologies as fast as untrained Mexicans.

My family and I stayed in Cuernavaca the rest of the year, and several students continued working in the lab with us during the fall of 1986. When we returned to Chicago in time for the holidays, the excavations were complete but less than one-quarter of the artifacts had been studied. I applied for, and received, a second grant from the National Science Foundation. This covered the costs of three more seasons of laboratory study in Cuernavaca, plus a few technical analyses.

We returned to the lab the following two summers and finally for six months in 1989. I hired back our old lab crew each year, and they classified more potsherds than me or the students. They also helped with many other tasks, from labeling artifacts to measuring them, and from note-taking to teaching Cindy and I to dance the *cumbia* at one of our season-end fiestas.

Hand-made tortillas

When asked about my favorite foods, I usually put hand-made tortillas near the top of the list. When women in small villages like Tetlama make tortillas by hand today, they are using just about the same method their Aztec ancestors used six centuries ago. First, a woman soaks the maize kernels in water along with limestone; this causes a chemical reaction that helps improve the nutritional content of the maize. This soaking almost certainly was done in some of the ceramic jars whose sherds we pulled out of every midden. After soaking overnight, women grind the maize into *masa* (coarse flour) on a hand grinder known as a *metate*. We recovered many fragments of *metates* that are identical to modern traditional *metates* in Tetlama and other central Mexican villages today. A *metate* has a flat or slightly concave rectangular platform, typically supported by three or four low feet. They are made of basalt, a volcanic lava that has numerous small holes that improve its grinding properties. A hand tool known today as a *mano*, also made of basalt, is used with the *metate*, and we found numerous fragments of these in the excavations.

Once the maize is ground, the next step is to form the tortillas by hand and toast them on a *comal* (griddle). *Comal* sherds were abundant in middens, and, like *metates* and *manos*, the Aztec period examples are nearly identical to the modern examples. These are very distinctive vessels: large circular, slightly concave platters with a smooth upper surface and a lower surface that has been deliberately roughened to improve heat transfer (Figure 3.4). In Mexican cities today, tortillas are made by machine and sold by the kilo. Women in traditional villages today (including Tetlama) either buy tortillas, or else make them from maize ground in a commercial mill. But on special occasions, village women still grind maize and form their tortillas by hand. There are few foods as delicious as a fresh, hand-made tortilla, toasted on a *comal*. Our scientific pursuit of ethnoarchaeology required that we participate in fiestas in Tetlama and eat hand-made tortillas (not to mention *mole* and other tasty foods). We did this partly to gain insight into Aztec food practices (really!) but mainly to enjoy Mexican food at its best. The women in Tetlama enjoyed teaching Cindy and our daughters how to make tortillas by hand, a skill that continues to pay off today.

Comals are large vessels, several feet in diameter. I had tried for years to get an intact *comal*—modern, not ancient—home from Mexico, with the only result being a growing collection of *comal* potsherds to show students. Many of our friends and

FIGURE 3.4 Women making and cooking tortillas. Drawing by Kagan McLeod.

compadres in Tetlama had family members in the nearby village of Cuentepec. Located at the end of a long dirt road, Cuentepec is one of the most isolated villages in Morelos, and many residents still speak Nahuatl. They also maintain a tradition of producing *comals*, which are sold in markets around the state. Cindy and I bought two Cuentepec *comals*, and we managed to get both of them back to the U.S. in our pickup truck, packed in big cartons between pillows. Unfortunately it is impossible to use a *comal* on an electric stove. We stored them in our laundry room, and I managed to break one while working on the dryer a few years ago. I don't think Cindy has ever forgiven me for that.

I used two methods to recover plant remains to prove the cultivation of maize, beans, and other crops. First, we took soil samples from the middens and processed them using a method known as "soil flotation." We would dump the soil into a large bin of water. Heavy items, such as stone and pottery, sink to the bottom. The soil itself dissolves into the water, and very light items float to the surface. These "floats" from the surface include tiny fragments of bone and any seeds that have been preserved. When seeds are partially burned in a fire they are converted to carbon, and carbonized seeds will last in the ground for centuries and float to the top during flotation. We processed hundreds of flotation samples, but only ended up with one or two beans and maize kernels. Either not many seeds were carbonized, or else they simply did not preserve well in the soils at Capilco and Cuexcomate.

While efforts to identify plant remains in the middens using flotation were not successful, I had better luck with a second method we applied to the check-dam fields where crops were grown: pollen analysis. A sample of soil is treated specially to extract microscopic pollen grains that can survive for many centuries in the ground. The check-dam soils contained pollen from maize, squash, prickly-pear cactus, and amaranth. The cactus, whose paddles and fruits were consumed (much as they still are in central Mexico), most likely grew at the edges of fields, while the other crops (plus beans and cotton) were grown in the check-dam plots. The pollen samples from the check-dam fields did not contain cotton pollen. Because of peculiarities in the nature of cotton pollen and how it gets dispersed by the wind, however, it is rarely present in agricultural fields where cotton was grown.

After the harvest, the maize cobs are allowed to dry, and then they are shelled and the dry kernels are stored for the year. We interpreted a number of circular features as wall foundations for a traditional form of maize granary called a *cuexcomatl* (this is the origin of the name of the site). Although our pollen and flotation studies of these features were inconclusive about their use for storage, this seems a reasonable hypothesis. Nevertheless, there were not enough of these granaries to go around, so some households must have stored their maize within the house.

The artifacts of daily life

Bones from a variety of animals turned up in our screens. People were evidently eating two domesticated species (turkey and dog) as well as wild game such as deer, rabbit, peccary, lizard, and turtle. Archaeologists identify animal species by comparing excavated bone fragments to a comparative collection of modern animal skeletons. This is done by specialists called "zooarchaeologists," which refers to the study of zoological material, not the excavation of zoos. Cindy had training in zooarchaeology at the University of Florida, and she identified our animal bones. Although we found a good variety of species, the numbers were very low. People were eating these domesticated and wild animals, but not very frequently. We also found cut marks on some turkey bones that showed people were making long hollow straw-like bone tubes, for some unknown use.

The middens contained other items used in food preparation and we have a good idea of the uses of some of these. For example, bowls or mortars made of basalt were probably used in a similar fashion to the way they are used today: to grind chilies and other foods to make guacamole and various sauces. The modern Mexican term for these—*molcajete*—is a variant of the original Nahuatl term, *molcaxitl*.

People used cutting tools of obsidian for a variety of domestic tasks, from food preparation to repairing farm tools. Obsidian is volcanic glass, and for the archaeologist it has three remarkable properties. First, the blades have extremely sharp edges; in fact they are the sharpest edge known to science, sharper than a surgeon's scalpel. (You can often identify the obsidian specialist in an archaeology lab by the bandages on his or her fingers.) Second, archaeologists can reconstruct the precise steps taken in manufacturing blades and other tools. This is because production proceeds by gradually removing tiny waste flakes until the tool is complete. The waste flakes removed at each stage of the process are different, which allows archaeologists to decipher the production sequence with great precision. The third remarkable property of this stone is that it occurs naturally in only a small number of places, and individual pieces can be matched to their source through chemical analysis.

To make cutting tools, the people of Capilco and Cuexcomate could easily have picked up cobbles of chert, a locally available stone found in fields around the sites. But instead they chose to purchase obsidian blades in the market. We know from the lack of waste flakes that the blades and other tools were not manufactured at these sites. The local chert could produce perfectly serviceable cutting tools, although not as sharp as obsidian. The abundance of obsidian coming out of the excavations was one of the first clues that the people of Capilco and Cuexcomate were well off economically.

At meals, food was served in pottery bowls. Many were painted with geometric patterns in red and black on a white background. They follow a set painting style found only in Morelos called the "Tlahuica polychrome style" (Figure 3.5, top). Also popular were serving vessels imported from the imperial heartland, the Valley of Mexico.

The fanciest serving vessels—bowls, pitchers, and cups—had a shiny red surface, often painted with black designs. Such vessels are even more abundant at sites in the Valley of Mexico, and my initial hunch was that our examples were imported. But chemical analyses (done later, for the Yautepec project), revealed the surprising result that about half of the polished red vessels were made locally and the rest imported. These ceramics show that Aztec styles from the imperial heartland were

FIGURE 3.5 Two kinds of ceramic vessel: a painted polychrome bowl from Cuexcomate, and three long-handled censers from an offering at Coatetelco, a nearby site. Photograph by Michael E. Smith.

understood out in the provinces. Overall, I was surprised at the large number of decorated vessels—and the diversity of imported vessels—found in every excavated trash deposit.

As we worked through the ceramic fragments in the lab, this kind of evidence for prosperous and well-furnished houses kept accumulating. When archaeologists find a few fancy vessels among a mass of plainware, we are tempted to compare it to modern fine china that is only brought out on very special occasions. But the elaborately decorated bowls, pitchers, and cups were so abundant that they seemed more comparable to today's everyday dishes.

One of the questions we wanted to answer was whether people produced craft items in their homes. The artifacts showed wide variation in the intensity of craft production. At one extreme sit the spinning tools described above: all households (that is, the women of all households) produced cloth. The knowledge and skills were widespread. No one made a living as a specialized spinner or weaver, and no one had to purchase cloth from the market. Obsidian blades sit at the opposite end of the scale: no one at Capilco and Cuexcomate manufactured obsidian blades or other tools. The nearly 10,000 tools we excavated must have been purchased at the market.

I found evidence for only one craft industry in the middle of the scale, between the polar opposites of cloth and obsidian: bark paper. People make bark paper today in some rural areas, and they paint it with colorful designs to sell to tourists.

Early Spanish writers described how the paper was produced at the time of the Spanish conquest. First, the bark is stripped from the wild fig tree and soaked in a stream. Then it is scraped to release its long fibers, which are pounded together to make the paper. Archaeological evidence for bark paper production consists of rectangular basalt objects called "bark beaters" that were used to pound the fibers. About the size of a cigarette pack, they have one flat side and one side with deep parallel grooves. We excavated thirty-three of these. Bark paper was used to create documents painted with glyphs, from ritual manuals for priests to tax lists for kings.

Access to markets

One of the most surprising results of my fieldwork in Morelos, at these sites and later at Yautepec, was the extent to which the Aztec market system reached into the provinces to provide households with the goods they needed. Obsidian is the most obvious import. The closest geological source of obsidian is more than 100 miles away. Ninety-five percent of our obsidian had a green tint, which indicates that it came from a specific source near the Mexican city of Pachuca.

The needles and other items of bronze were obvious imports, and it turns out they were smuggled goods, bought on the black market. The technology for smelting copper with tin or arsenic to produce bronze was invented some 2,000 years ago in South America, independent of the Old World. Research by Dorothy Hosler revealed that the technology was then brought by seafaring merchants up the Pacific coast to Mexico, sometime between AD 500 and 1000, where the technology flourished in the western Mexican states of Michoacan and Jalisco. Although people in several parts of the Mexica Empire had started to experiment with smelting in the final century before the arrival of Cortés, most bronze items in central Mexico were obtained by trade from western Mexico (Hosler 1994).

As the leading expert on the bronze artifacts of ancient Mesoamerica, Dorothy has analyzed thousands of bronze artifacts in museum collections all over Mexico. By examining cross-sections of artifacts under a special microscope, she could determine how they were made. She refined her understanding of bronze smelting by having her undergraduate classes at Massachusetts Institute of Technology re-create ancient smelting methods in the laboratory. She found that ancient artisans had deliberately varied the composition of the metal to achieve particular goals. For example, by changing the percentage of tin in small bronze bells, they made them look golden.

Dorothy was excited about our fifty-one bronze artifacts because this was the first batch of such items to come from well-dated contexts, excavated with modern methods. The many bronze artifacts in museums were either looted from burials or else excavated in early days when archaeologists did not keep detailed notes.

Surprisingly, our results showed that bronze tools were a regular part of commoner toolkits, and not something used only by nobles and priests. Although we excavated a noble's residence at Cuexcomate, nearly all of the bronze items came from commoner middens. Not only was bronze an imported good, it was contraband, obtained through the black market. Most production zones were inside the Tarascan Empire, the major enemy of the Mexica Empire. According to Mexica nobles (and the historians who rely on their testimony), no commerce crossed the fortified border between these two states. Thus the transport of bronze into Aztec territory during the Imperial Period must have been done outside of official channels, through the black market. Smuggling goods across political borders is nothing new. The bronze needles, bells, and other items I excavated at these sites are proof of a hidden part of the economy that would remain unknown if scholars relied only on the historical record.

I cannot claim to be the first to describe smuggling across the Mexica-Tarascan border. Gary Jennings, in his bestselling novel, *Aztec*, has smugglers carrying goods back and forth across the border (Jennings 1980). While a novelist's plot is no substitute for real evidence, Jennings deserves credit for identifying the likelihood of smuggling at a time when archaeologists and historians refused to consider it (Smith 2001).

We found even smaller numbers of other exotic goods from many hundreds of miles away. The most impressive of these are beads made of jadeite. Jadeite or greenstone is a hard, fine stone used for jewelry in most Mesoamerican cultures, and it is often called "jade." Geologists have now located the major geological source used by the Classic Maya in Guatemala, and it is likely that Aztec jadeite came from this location as well (Helferich 2011).

After obsidian the most plentiful imported goods were ceramic vessels. In many cases it is easy to recognize pots made in different areas. Each region of central Mexico specialized in a particular style of painted pottery. Most of the painted vessels used by a household were of the local style, with a small number of decorated pots from other areas. People regularly used plates and spinning bowls traded from the Valley of Mexico. Decorated bowls from other parts of the state of Morelos and from adjacent regions were also abundant. The presence of so many foreign goods shows that the people of Capilco and Cuexcomate were well connected within both the economic and social networks of Aztec central Mexico. They were not poor, isolated peasants; they were wealthy, well-connected farmers.

The hidden realm of domestic ritual

The people of Capilco and Cuexcomate did not devote all their time to farming, cooking, and economic activities; they also had a rich ceremonial life. The ritual objects we found in the middens diverge from standard accounts of Aztec public religion. The works of the Spanish friars are full of detailed descriptions of Aztec myths, gods, and public ceremonies that ranged from ritual dances to human sacrifices. Out in the countryside we find few traces of public religion, yet the middens are full of objects used in ritual and ceremony.

Many rituals began with sap from copal tree. This sap releases a pleasant scent when burned, and the Aztecs believed this scent allowed communication with the gods. Copal incense is still used in Mexico today in churches. Every household had one or more censers for burning copal during domestic rites. These shallow ceramic bowls look like frying pans, with long, hollow tubes for handles (Figure 3.5, bottom). They are identical to censers used by priests in public rituals at the imperial capital Tenochtitlan. Perhaps they signal some kind of connection between Aztec public religion and domestic rituals.

But another common item used in domestic ritual—ceramic figurines—had no counterpart in the world of Aztec public religion. Figurines are small clay images of people, animals, and gods, and they are almost completely absent from offerings at temples. Most figurines depict people, and many writers on Aztec religion have assumed they must be images of gods. Many pages have been filled with debates about the precise identification of these gods. Is this Quetzalcoatl, or maybe Tlaloc? Or could it be Xipe Totec? The problem is that the figurine images do not look like the gods. With a few exceptions, they lack the specific items of clothing, headdresses, and cult items that identify Aztec gods. Although a small number of figurines clearly do depict gods, most do not. To me, the fact that figurines depict people rather than gods is a clue to their use. They were not used in public rituals dedicated to the high gods. Instead, they were used by women in ceremonies of curing and divination that took place within the home (Smith 2002). This domain is hardly mentioned in the writings of the Spanish friars.

Ceramic figurines point up some of the biases in the standard written accounts of Aztec religion. The Spanish friars talked mostly to noblemen, not commoners. Moreover, the friars never entered commoner homes and they had little contact with women of any social class. The home was the domain of women, and Aztec women were considered dangerous by the friars. The secret world of domestic ritual is almost invisible in the historical record, and it is up to archaeology to bring these household ceremonies to light again.

Musical instruments are another kind of ritual object used in the homes at Capilco and Cuexcomate. Although rarer than censers and figurines, ceramic flutes, rattles, and whistles turned up in most middens. I didn't realize how surprising these finds were until several years later when I was talking with the German archaeologist Adje Both, the leading scholar of Aztec music and musical instruments. When the friars talked about music and instruments, it was always in the context of public, state-sponsored ceremonies. Adje and others had no idea that commoners (much less peasants) had musical instruments in their homes. When I first told Adje about these finds, he was skeptical—what would these instruments be doing in peasant middens? So I sent him photos and drawings, and he got excited and wanted to examine the objects himself. I later arranged for him to come to Mexico and study our collections. We cannot say for sure whether people used these items in their domestic ceremonies, or brought them out for the occasional public celebration, or both. But it is exciting to imagine that their homes may have been filled with music, even if only on special occasions.

Rich and poor

My excavations provided the first direct comparison between the lifestyles of Aztec commoners and nobles. The Aztec nobility was an exclusive club, less than five percent of the population. To be a noble, you had to be born to noble parents, and your rights and privileges were spelled out in legal codes. You could only marry another noble (although noblemen often had commoner concubines). Members of your group owned all the land, and they controlled the city-state government. Even if you were the lowest ranking noble in town, you enjoyed more wealth and power than commoners.

These features of the Aztec nobility were borne out in the architecture of Group 6 at Cuexcomate. This compound differed tremendously from the mass of commoner houses at the site. Instead of small, rectangular buildings constructed at the level of the ground, Group 6 consisted of a series of connected platforms arranged around a central patio with a single entrance (Figure 3.6). Stone foundations for rooms sat on top of the platforms. The stonework included many cut stones instead of the river cobbles used in commoner houses, and the floors and walls were covered with white lime plaster.

Group 6 was too large and complex to excavate completely, so we dug a trench through the main structure to examine the stratigraphy (layering of deposits). Under the main platform we found evidence for two earlier stages of construction. First the soil was cleared away during the initial construction of the platform. Then several layers of trash built up on the ground surface as people lived in the structure for decades and tossed their trash out back. Next, a jumble of rocks, plaster, and debris from the destruction or deterioration of the structure covered the midden. Finally, modern plowing had churned up the top portion of the debris layer.

If we apply modern aesthetic judgments, I'd say the inhabitants of Group 6 were slobs. They tossed their trash out back, to build up outside the house, just like the commoners at the site. But from the perspective of household archaeology, I thank them for leaving their garbage where we could find it. During excavation, the artifacts from this midden did not seem to differ greatly from what we were pulling out of the commoner houses. When we got to the lab, I was very interested to see just how the material would compare.

In most ways the "elite trash" was just like the "commoner trash," with the same kinds of turkey bones, tortilla griddles, and spindle whorls. The major difference was that the residents of Group 6 had more decorated bowls and more imported vessels. This difference was measurable (and statistically significant), but it was not extreme. There were no artifact categories found exclusively in elite contexts. The most valuable items—bronze needles, jadeite beads and other jewelry, the fanciest pottery—were available to both commoners and elites at these sites. So the lifestyles of the rich and famous at Cuexcomate were not all that different from the lifestyles of the rest of society. Yes, these nobles used greater quantities of fancy serving pottery, but that is about the extent of the differences in their artifacts. They did live in a much larger and better-built house, though. Perhaps these similarities between noble and commoner trash can be explained by the fact

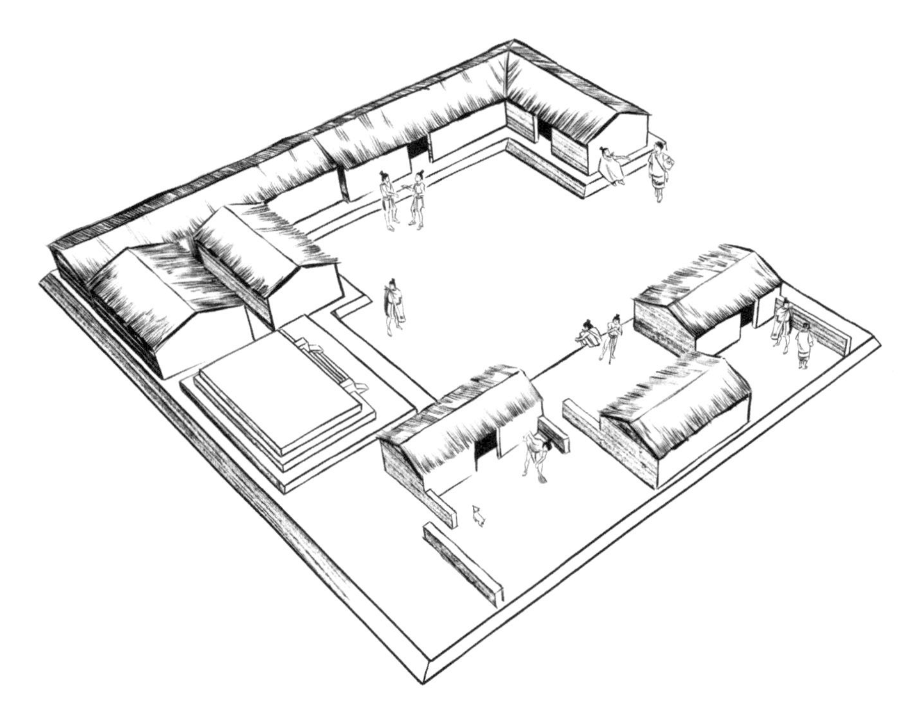

FIGURE 3.6 The elite compound at Cuexcomate in the Growth Period, Group 6. Drawing by Kagan McLeod.

that the inhabitants of Group 6 were rather low-ranking nobles within the Aztec hierarchy. Maybe the trash from a royal palace would be something else entirely.

Changes in rural society

The kinds of houses and terraces people built, and the kinds of artifacts they used, did not change greatly during the 400-plus years of the Aztec period in the Buenavista hills. But life and history were not static. I knew from historical sources that the Mexica Empire had conquered this region around AD 1430, and one of my fieldwork goals was to identify the impact of that conquest. With considerable time and effort I worked out the time line shown in Figure 3.7. Chronology-building, I'm afraid, is not the most exciting branch of archaeology, and I will spare the reader the gory details of how I managed to create this time line.[3] During my student days, the shortest relevant archaeological time period, called the "Late Aztec Period" lasted from 1350 until the Spanish conquest of 1521. But the Mexica Empire was founded and started expanding in the middle of that interval (in 1428), which made it impossible to compare conditions before and after imperial conquest. With my new chronology I could investigate the effects of Mexica conquest on provincial society for the first time.

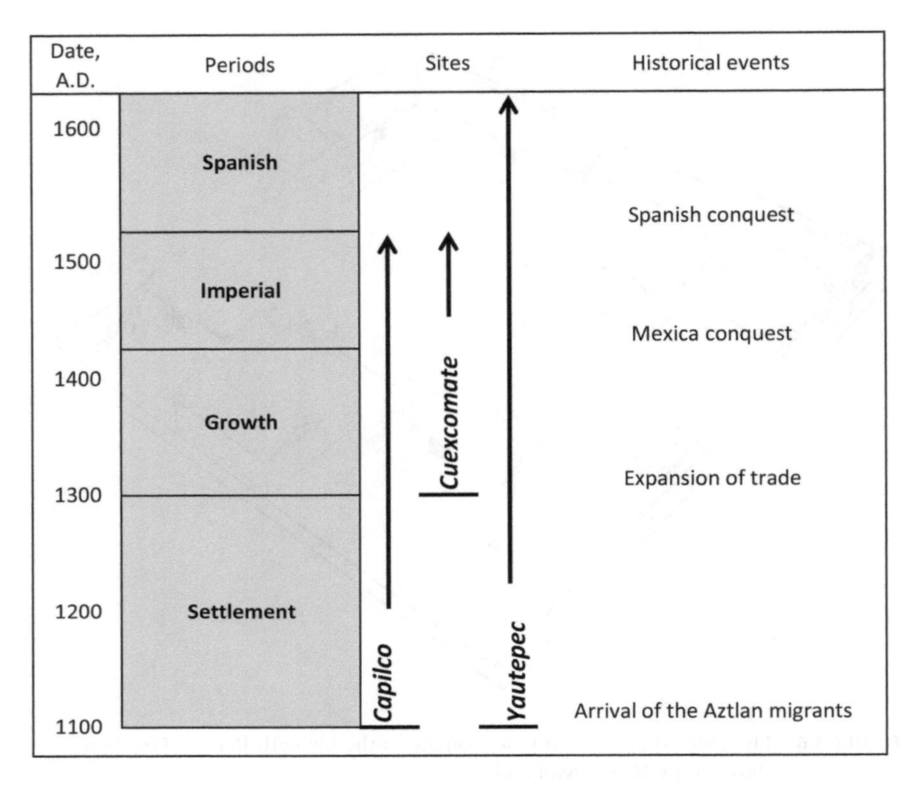

FIGURE 3.7 Time line, showing the four periods of occupation and major historical events.

At the start of the project my colleagues and I had expected to see major changes in society, including a big drop in the standard of living and an end to economic growth as people started paying heavy taxes to the empire. We thought the Mexica Empire was an exploitative regime that conquered provincial peoples and then bled them dry with taxes.

One of the first signs that these expectations were off base came when we applied the new chronology to the excavated houses. The results are quite remarkable: once a house was built and occupied, it was not abandoned until the Spanish conquest. If conditions were made so miserable by Mexica conquest, I would expect some people to move away and try their fortune elsewhere. They could have followed the age-old peasant response to economic crisis and moved into a city, or they could have moved to the remote areas along the southwest border of the empire. But people stayed at Capilco and Cuexcomate, with a single exception: the large noble house at Cuexcomate—Group 6—was abandoned and left in ruins during the Imperial Period.

As our artifact studies moved forward, it became increasingly clear that my initial expectations were not at all correct. The changes from the Growth to Imperial periods turned out to be quite minor. If I did not know from historical documents that this area had been conquered in the 1430s, I'm not sure I could identify imperial conquest from the excavations alone. Could the Mexica Empire really have been such a minor force? My colleagues and I started asking what it was about Mexica imperialism that led to such a minor impact on provincial society. I now realize that this was the wrong question. Instead of asking what was *wrong* with the empire, a better idea is to ask what was *right* with provincial society. That is: was there something about the households and communities in Morelos that shielded them from being destroyed or exploited by the Mexica?

Notes

1 Archaeologists worked out the use of spindle whorls to spin thread over a century ago. The uses of spinning bowls was something I figured out in my dissertation research; see Smith and Hirth (1988). For more information on Aztec textiles and the artifacts used to make them, see Berdan (1987), or Smith (2012: 87–92).
2 The artifacts from these sites are described in Smith (2015a).
3 The chronology for Capilco and Cuexcomate is described in Smith and Doershuk (1991). The Settlement Period corresponds to the Temazcalli phase, the Growth Period to the Early Cuauhnahuac phase, and the Imperial Period is the Late Cuauhnahuac phase.

4

A HIGH QUALITY OF LIFE

Breakthroughs in understanding come in many different forms. For archaeologists, the discovery of King Tut's tomb in Egypt and the uncovering of the Aztec "Templo Mayor" in Mexico City overturned existing knowledge. As someone doing household archaeology, however, my breakthroughs are far less spectacular, and they usually come only after all the artifacts have been studied. By the end of our four seasons of laboratory analysis in Cuernavaca, it seemed pretty clear that the people whose houses I excavated had been wealthy and well-connected. But how did these ancient Aztec farmers manage to achieve a high quality of life, and how did they maintain it for centuries? My answer to these questions had to wait for two more advances of a very different sort: conceptual breakthroughs. The first was made by a group of Aztec specialists at a summer workshop on the Mexica Empire in 1986. The second conceptual breakthrough took me much longer to achieve—a new understanding of how Aztec communities created and promoted the prosperity and quality of life of their members. It required another excavation project—Yautepec—and the discovery of new historical documents before the pieces fell into place.

Wealthy households

The houses of the rich and famous at Cuexcomate—the nobles in Group 6—differed from their commoner subjects, what about the artifacts? I read study after study about household possessions and wealth levels by historians and anthropologists. They all came to the same conclusion: household goods differ greatly between rich and poor. While this might not sound very surprising, we can't always assume that conditions in other societies match those of our own society. Just how do artifacts vary with wealth? Among reindeer hunters in arctic Finland, everybody has a snowmobile, but only the wealthiest families have a television. In Mexico City, household wealth can be predicted just by examining the furniture. And in the New England colonies before the Revolution, you could tell the better-off families simply by looking at their tea set.

The best of these studies is a series of reports by sociologists working in rural Oklahoma in the 1940s. William H. Sewell and his colleagues were given the task of measuring the wealth and standard of living of Oklahoma farm families to help federal and state agencies protect and promote agriculture in the wake of the Great Depression (Figure 4.1). Working in the era before government tracking of economic statistics, Sewell and his colleagues had to find creative ways to measure standard of living. So they went out to the farms, observed the premises, and talked to the families. Sewell worked out a quantitative scale based on income, housing, possessions, and the participation of family members in group activities.

I found myself in a similar situation with respect to the Morelos households, so I turned to Sewell's work in Oklahoma for inspiration. If houses and possessions were good measures of wealth and standard of living in twentieth-century, rural Oklahoma, why wouldn't they serve for houses and artifacts from rural Aztec Mexico? As it turns out, an archaeological version of Sewell's standard of living scale worked very well at my sites. Instead of asking about the type of bathroom in the house, or the presence of a tractor in the barn, I could ask about the size

FIGURE 4.1 Photograph of an Oklahoma farm family in 1942. Photo by Alfred Eisenstaedt/Getty Images. Reproduced with permission.

of houses and the quantities of imported pottery. The noble house (Group 6) was twenty times larger than the average commoner house, a fact consistent with Sewell's scale that also accords with basic common sense.

I set out to measure household wealth using artifacts from the middens. My reading had shown that the best way to measure wealth with artifacts is to focus on the number of high-value goods at each house (Smith 1987), so I focused on imported goods (obsidian, bronze, and imported ceramics) and painted ceramic vessels used for serving food and drink. These wealth-related artifacts showed two things. First, the commoner households were relatively well-off in comparison to their cousins at other ancient communities in Mesoamerica. And second, nobles had greater numbers of high-value goods than commoners. They did not have a monopoly on items like greenstone jewelry or bronze needles, but they had more imported goods and more painted pottery than their commoner subjects.

Household choice and the diversity of goods

Just about everyone would agree that wealth, or economic level, is only one component of living a good life. In the words of three economists, "Quality of life is a broader concept than economic production and living standards. It includes the full range of factors that influences what we value in living, reaching beyond its material side" (Stiglitz et al. 2010: 61). One of those economists, Amartya Sen, won the 1998 Nobel Prize in Economics in part for his studies of the non-economic aspects of the quality of life in the developing world. Sen evidently did not realize he was repeating an earlier breakthrough. Sewell and his colleagues in Oklahoma had already discovered the concept of quality of life, and devised ways to measure it, decades earlier. Three of Sewell's measures—housing, possessions, and income—were economic indicators of the standard of living, while one of his categories—the participation of family members in community activities—went beyond economics in promoting a high quality of life (Belcher 1951; Sewell 1940). These sociologists used the term "level of living" for the economic part of quality of life, and the term "socio-economic status" for the non-economic part.

Although he cannot be credited with first identifying the non-economic aspects of the quality of life, Amartya Sen did provide the best account of these factors. In his scheme, prosperity is not just about having resources. It also involves the freedom of individuals to exercise their human "capabilities" to achieve the goals they value. Sen's approach has been taken up by the United Nations in its Human Development Index that monitors economic development and its human impacts in countries around the world (Phillips 2006; Sen 1992).

Building on the work of Sewell and Sen, I devised two ways to measure the non-economic component of the quality of life with archaeological remains: first, a great diversity of goods in each domestic midden, and second, people participating in social networks that extended beyond their local communities (Smith 2016b). These two advantages enabled the people of Capilco and Cuexcomate to achieve a good quality of life. The accompanying box shows the diversity of goods I excavated at almost every house.

Basic goods of an Aztec household in Morelos

Food preparation items. Obsidian knives, a metate to grind corn, a stone mortar, ceramic vessels to prepare food (bowls, jars, and basins), baskets and salt vessels. People living along the salty lakes in the Valley of Mexico produced salt by evaporating the water. They packed the salt into distinctive jars with a rough finish and shipped it out to the provinces. The residents of Capilco and Cuexcomate then purchased these jars of salt. As they used up the salt, people broke pieces off the jar (to better get at the remaining salt), and these sherds are abundant in all the middens.

Ceramic serving vessels. Serving bowls (unpainted orange dishes, and bowls painted in colorful geometric designs), drinking cups, and pitchers.

Tools for craft production. Spindle whorls, spinning bowls, sewing needles, molds, scrapers, and polishers for making fired clay objects, bark beaters for making paper, and pigment stones to make the paint for pictorial manuscripts.

Weapons. Arrow points of obsidian and chert, and small marble-sized ceramic balls used as pellets in blow-guns for hunting birds and other small animals.

Ritual items. Two forms of censers, figurines, musical instruments, tobacco pipes, ceramic sculptures, quartz crystals, and small bronze jingle bells.

Jewelry. Lip plugs of obsidian and rock crystal, ear spools of obsidian and fired clay, and pendants or beads made of jadeite, rock crystal, shell, and tweezers made of bronze, which Dorothy Hosler's research had revealed as ceremonial jewelry.

Owning multiple types of object in various categories does not seem strange to us today. Cindy and I can eat dinner using any of several sets of dishes, including fine china, Mexican ceramic dishes, and paper plates. My toolbox has four pairs of pliers and even more screwdrivers, and Cindy has many different pieces of jewelry. But for peasant households in the Mexica Empire this kind of diversity was a remarkable finding. Household members had considerable choice as to what item to use for any task. If a woman was planning a ceremony to cure someone, she could choose to use figurines, censers, musical instruments, or quartz crystals. To serve turkey and bean tacos for dinner, a family could use a plain bowl, a locally made painted bowl, or a painted bowl imported from a distant area. The residents of the excavated houses were able to exercise a number of different human capabilities, to use Amartya Sen's term. They were not limited to one way of doing things, but could choose among a range of options.

An even more important way that people could exercise their capabilities was to participate in social networks that linked them to the outside world.

External social networks

Cuexcomate and Capilco were not isolated settlements. Outsiders introduced taxes, war, and exploitation to the Buenavista hills, but they also brought trade, wealth, and expanded opportunities. How did these positive and negative forces balance out? I begin with two external social networks that were open to commoners and nobles alike: the market system and artifact style networks. These connections brought new goods and new ideas, all of which promoted the capabilities of each household.

Cindy and I witnessed firsthand the importance of external social networks in raising the quality of life of peasant farmers. Our formal compadre bonds with people in Tetlama were just this sort of link. Our relationships with these families included low levels of economic support, and the bonds we formed set up expectations for the future. Our compadres could call on us in times of need. My family was thus an outside resource for a few families in Tetlama. The compadre bond is a kind of network relationship that links Tetlama residents with the outside world (Mintz and Wolf 1950).

The market system

Today we buy things in stores or online. For in-person shopping, we may go to a mall, or to a busy downtown shopping district, because that allows us to visit several stores in a single trip. In Aztec times, people accomplished the same thing by going to their local marketplace on market day. Market day came once a week in most Aztec communities—that is, every five days, as an Aztec month contained twenty days divided into four weeks of five days each. Markets were not just economic outlets; market day was an important social occasion. People went to the marketplace to see friends, eat a taco, and catch up on the latest gossip. Cuexcomate probably had a weekly market that met in the central plaza (Figure 4.2).

People used two kinds of money to make purchases in the market. Cotton cloth of a set size served for large purchases, while cacao (chocolate) beans were small change used to buy a taco or some tomatoes. One piece of cloth was worth between 60 and 300 cacao beans. These two items resembled modern money in many ways, but there was one big difference: money could not purchase land or labor. The Aztecs had a commercial economy (that is, an economy based on money and markets), but it was not a capitalist economy. It's good to keep in mind that although commercial economies—with money and markets—seem natural to most people today, not all ancient economies fit this model. The Incas of Peru and ancient Egyptians had "command economies" in which the government ran the economy. They did not have money, markets, or merchants; instead, bureaucrats ran things.

Marketplaces not too different from those in Aztec times still flourish in most Mexican cities and towns today. We did a fair amount of shopping for food in the Cuernavaca central marketplace, which was located only a few blocks from our house. This is a large roofed space filled with many hundreds of small, individually run stalls. Vendors specialize in a particular type of product, and the stalls selling each type of good are located close together. Bargaining is a major part of many transactions in modern Mexican marketplaces, just as it had been in Aztec times. As foreigners, Cindy and I would normally be charged higher prices than local residents. We tried to bargain, but didn't make much progress. When we complained about this to our compadres in Tetlama, Pedro Ramírez offered to help us out. Vendors in a market often establish special relationships with particular buyers. In return for getting a better price, the buyer would return to the same stall with his or her business. Pedro introduced us to his regular meat seller.

"These are my compadres," he said, "so please treat them like you treat me. They could be good customers here, even if they are gringos." Most Americans who come to the Cuernavaca market are tourists, only interested in blankets, jewelry, and other such goods. If they wandered into the food area, they rarely stopped to buy anything.

"Yes, of course! I wouldn't think of charging your compadres higher prices! You are my valued customer, and now they are too." We did get better prices from this vendor than we had paid originally, but I'm pretty sure he charged us more than he charged his regular Mexican customers like our compadre Pedro.

The largest marketplace in the Mexica Empire, by far, was in Tlatelolco, the northern sector of the imperial capital Tenochtitlan. In the words of the conquistador Bernal Díaz del Castillo:

> On reaching the market-place . . . we were astounded at the great number of people and the quantities of merchandise, and at the orderliness and good arrangement that prevailed, for we had never seen such a thing. . . . You could see every kind of merchandise to be found anywhere in New Spain.
>
> *(Díaz del Castillo 1963: 232)*

This central Aztec market was important for the people of Morelos because it reigned over a network of marketplaces that covered all of central Mexico. Some cotton cloth produced in Morelos households eventually made its way to the Tlatelolco market. Merchants linked many hundreds of local markets into a single network. Without these connections, exotic goods like bronze needles or Tarascan obsidian would not have found their way into the middens we excavated.

Professional merchants known as *pochteca* traded in the markets, and they ran the one at Tlatelolco. The pochteca were organized into a guild with restricted membership. They traveled all over Mesoamerica, both within the empire and into enemy territory. Some pochteca made huge fortunes and became wealthier than many nobles. They also served as spies for the emperor in enemy lands. Regional merchants, who were not members of the pochteca guild, also traveled among central Mexican markets. Most of the people selling in the markets, however, were not professional merchants but petty vendors—commoners selling their family's produce or craft goods in small amounts. When Hernan Cortés described the Tlatelolco market—with awe and amazement at its size and complexity—he mentioned the many hundreds of small individual stalls, arranged in groups by the type of goods sold—just like the Cuernavaca market today. The thousands of

FIGURE 4.2 Market day at Cuexcomate. Drawing by Kagan McLeod.

obsidian objects I found in domestic middens were probably all purchased in the market from household-level producer-vendors. The markets relied on money, and barter was rare. Lists of market sales at the time of the Spanish Conquest tell us that an obsidian blade, for example, cost five cacao beans and sixteen blades could be purchased for one piece of cotton money-cloth.

Like peasant market systems in Mexico and other developing countries today, Aztec markets were periodic—that is, each market met on a particular day of the five-day Aztec week, and nearby market schedules were coordinated. This allowed merchants to travel from market to market, stopping at each on its designated day. Periodic market systems make good economic sense: for merchants they extend the area of demand for their goods, and for consumers the weekly market offers a wider range of goods than would be possible if markets met daily. And periodic markets also make good social sense, providing a weekly focus for community gatherings and interaction.

Cindy and I experienced the social side of periodic markets many times during our years of living in Mexico. While still graduate students, we spent several seasons working on artifacts in the picturesque village of Tepoztlan. The sixteenth-century convent, a tourist destination today, was used to store artifacts, including the collections of our friend Ken Hirth. We had tables and lamps set up in an old monk's cell, where we sorted potsherds. Six days a week, the local Tepoztlan market occupied a special building next to the main plaza. But Sunday was market day. Trade moved out of the market building, and vendors set up awnings throughout the plaza and nearby streets. They sold everything from fresh vegetables to prepared food, and from hardware to tourist trinkets. Being diligent graduate students, we sometimes went into the lab on Sunday, when it took much longer just to get through the market to arrive at the convent's entrance. All over Mexico, market day is fun, just as it was in Aztec times. People in the communities described in this book experienced both the economic and the social benefits that came from their participation in the market system.

Being stylish in the countryside

Goods purchased in the marketplace were not the only kind of foreign influence on the people of Cuexcomate and Capilco. New ideas and concepts from distant cities also arrived in this rural area. People wanted to keep up with the latest styles from Tenochtitlan and the other big Aztec cities. Many of the objects in commoner middens shared elements of style with comparable items at Aztec sites in the Valley of Mexico and elsewhere. Ceramic figurines are a good example. In the lab, we divided figurines into three categories: some were made in a local style not found outside of Morelos; some were imported from the cities of the Valley of Mexico; and the largest group were made from local clays, but in the style of figurines from the Valley of Mexico. Clearly this style of figurine was important to people in the provinces. They bought some examples from merchants and then started making their own in the same style (Figure 4.3). Beyond figurines, many objects—from musical instruments to metates to censers—resembled things in the Valley of Mexico and other parts of central Mexico. People wanted to keep up with the latest styles, and they were able to do so.

Nobles were not exempt from this striving to stay stylish. The civic architecture at Cuexcomate shows that the nobles who lived in Group 6 participated in the elite social networks of central Mexico. The layout of Group 6 itself followed the standard plan of Aztec palaces. More dramatic, however, is the layout of the entire Cuexcomate epicenter. This layout corresponds to the "Tula plaza plan." Aztec kings expressed their legitimacy and power by designing their civic centers in imitation of the great ancient city of Tula, the pre-Aztec capital of central Mexico (Smith 2008). They put the largest temple on the east side of a large square plaza, with palaces, ballcourts, and other civic buildings on the other sides of the plaza. By laying out the town center of Cuexcomate—a rural town—as a small-scale version of larger Aztec cities, our noble was using architectural style and layout to make claims of status, legitimacy, and connections to more powerful realms. This was a rather bold architectural statement by a provincial rural lord, who was proclaiming his place at the table of the Aztec nobility.

These and other foreign styles at Capilco and Cuexcomate are evidence of active contacts and communication with distant areas. And in line with Amartya

FIGURE 4.3 Ceramic figurines from Yautepec. Drawing by Ben Karis.

Sen's concept of the quality of life, such contacts increased the choices, the options, and the capabilities of individual households. But before things begin to look too rosy, we need to look at a powerful negative force that impacted the households of Morelos: the Mexica Empire.

Aztec summer camp

An event called "Aztec summer camp" was the setting for one of the conceptual breakthroughs mentioned earlier: a new understanding of how the Mexica Empire worked. This summer workshop changed how I thought about the excavated sites and their role in Mexica Empire—twice.

After completing the excavations at Cuexcomate in 1986, I headed to Washington, DC, to attend the "camp"—our informal name for a summer workshop held at Dumbarton Oaks, a research center in historic Georgetown. The combined hard work of six Aztec specialists that summer produced a new map of the Mexica Empire and a breakthrough in understanding its organization. We published an influential book, *Aztec Imperial Strategies*. This experience changed how I thought about the Mexica Empire for more than two decades. But I later realized that the Dumbarton Oaks project had set me on the wrong track for understanding the remarkable households and communities I had excavated, and I later had to rethink where they fit in the wider world of Aztec period Mesoamerica.

Dumbarton Oaks specializes in three subjects: Byzantine Studies, Landscape Architecture, and Pre-Columbian Studies. Set in a former private mansion with extensive formal gardens, Dumbarton Oaks boasts the best library in the U.S. on its three topics. Scholars from all over the world come to study and write in its attractive setting. The new map our group produced that summer was truly a joint effort by six collaborating scholars.[1] When not working in the library, we enjoyed swimming in the formal pool and playing volleyball. Our group, however, was a bit too exuberant for the Director of Dumbarton Oaks. Although the groundskeeper said we would not hurt the formal lawn with our volleyball games, the Director did not want frivolous activities on the lawn and we had to move our games to a nearby city park. He strongly disapproved of the T-shirts we printed up with the Aztec calendar glyph for 1986 and the label "Aztec Summer Camp, Dumbarton Oaks." In a move reminiscent of high school, we were called into the Director's office and informed that Dumbarton Oaks was a serious institution; it was *not* a summer camp! But one reason for the success of our (very scholarly and serious) research was the fun we had while working as a team. I have to admit I felt guilty living it up at Dumbarton Oaks that summer while Cindy was back in Cuernavaca caring for two young girls while supervising the backfilling of our excavations. I think I still owe her.

The major contribution of the Dumbarton Oaks group was to identify Mexica polices of indirect control and map their occurrence throughout the empire. It was only natural that I should apply these insights to the excavated sites to interpret the archaeological remains. I came out of Aztec summer camp thinking that the ties between my sites and the imperial capital must have been the result of imperial policy.

I now realize that the Dumbarton Oaks project had in fact hindered my understanding of the sites in Morelos. I asked the question, why did the Mexica conquest of Morelos have so little effect on local society? After the Dumbarton Oaks project, the answer my colleagues and I gave focused on the empire: the imperial rulers simply had no need or desire to make changes in the provinces. The empire relied on indirect control of its provinces, which means that local rulers and institutions were left in place. The empire simply did not meddle very much in provincial affairs.

It took me years to realize that this was the wrong way to look at the imperial conquest of Morelos. I found in the works of economists Samuel Bowles, Herbert Gintis, Elinor Ostrom, and Amartya Sen a new bottom-up social perspective that finally allowed me to understand the importance of local conditions in Morelos. It was the local setting—things like terracing, cotton cultivation, and the way communities were organized—and not the policies of the distant imperial capital, that shaped the lives of these people and the ways they interacted with the empire.[2] The residents of Cuexcomate, Capilco, and Yautepec were somehow able to resist imperial conquest. In other words, they were resilient to outside intervention. A big part of the explanation lies in the fact that the relevant government for local affairs was the city-state, not the Mexica Empire.

The city-state was the major form of government in central Mexico during the Aztec period. A city-state was ruled by a hereditary king. People paid taxes to their king in money (cotton textiles), goods (grains, pots, other items) and labor. Because of its small size, people had a close relationship with their city-state. Aztec city-states resembled other city-state systems through history, from ancient Mesopotamia to Classical Greece to the Yoruba city-states of Africa. This was a successful and effective form of local rule in the premodern world. The word *local* is crucial here: by forging a successful local government, people in the provinces helped insulate themselves from the detrimental effects of conquest by the Mexica Empire.

The Mexica imperial protection racket

The great social historian Charles Tilly famously compared governments to organized crime (Tilly 1985). Following Tilly, the Mexica Empire was an early example of a protection racket. The message to the provinces was: Pay up or we will beat you up! The indirect rule of provinces by the Mexica Empire has always been difficult to understand. We often look to the Roman and British empires as the models of imperialism, empires that relied largely on direct rule. They destroyed local regimes, sent troops and administrators to the provinces, built cities and roads, and really tried to control things in provincial areas. Indirect rule, on the other hand, relies on local rulers to collect taxes, keep the peace, and run the provinces. Local rulers and elites were given privileges and benefits in exchange for their cooperation. This kind of empire, however, does not loom so large in the public imagination today.

Until recently many Aztec specialists believed that the Mexica Empire was a powerful and dominating state that ruled its territory with an iron fist. One of the goals of my excavations was to evaluate the effects of Mexica conquest on provincial society by comparing conditions before and after imperial conquest. Believing the empire was very powerful, I was sure that imperial conquest must have affected these communities greatly, and I was on the lookout for signs of destruction and decline in the Imperial Period. I was baffled and disappointed when the evidence showed that Mexica conquest had only minor effects on the people who lived in these sites. What was wrong with this picture?

A new theory of direct and indirect rule published in 2011 by a group of political scientists helped me see the situation from a different angle. John Gerring and his colleagues examined many cases of political control—from ancient empires to the U.S. occupation of Iraq—and concluded that the primary factor that accounts for the type of rule (direct or indirect) is the "degree of political organization" in the subordinate society (Gerring et al. 2011). If the area to be controlled already has a functioning government, then indirect control works best. But if the area is disorganized politically, it will require the personnel and resources of direct control. The key, then, is the nature of provincial society and government, not some grand imperial policy to use indirect rule or direct rule.

In the Aztec case, city-states had been functioning in Morelos for several centuries, which—according to Gerring's analysis—allowed the empire to set up indirect forms of control. Gerring's new theory helps explain the fact that different parts of the Mexica Empire were administered in different fashions: those with established and well-working city-states (like Morelos) were ruled indirectly, while those whose local governments were less organized—or destroyed by conquest—had to be ruled more directly, often by officials and garrisons sent from Tenochtitlan. But why were the Morelos city-states effective and successful? This question required more research, both archaeological and historical, and I will provide an answer in Chapter 7.

The new theory of indirect rule helps shift our attention from the capital to the provinces. How did provincial peoples—such as the residents of Capilco, Cuexcomate—view the Mexica Empire? What was its impact on their lives? These people paid imperial taxes, yet they received almost nothing in return, beyond a rather low level of protection. Remarkably, people were paying to be shielded not from enemies, but from the empire itself! The Mexica Empire was really just a big protection racket, not so different from modern organized crime in the way it exploits small businesses. Pay your taxes, the argument went, and we will refrain from invading your territory again. Needless to say, provincial peoples greatly resented the Mexica Empire, a situation that Cortés would use to his own advantage during his conquest of Mexico.

Imperial taxes were organized by province, and the goods owed by each province were depicted in colorful painted manuscripts.[3] The *Codex Mendoza* (Berdan and Anawalt 1992) is a copy of an original Aztec imperial tax list, painted a few decades after the Spanish conquest. One section of the document contains the imperial tax roll (Figure 4.4). The listing for each province starts with the head town, the place where taxes from the province were assembled for shipment to Tenochtitlan. In this example, the glyph for the head town (Huaxtepec) is listed at the top left. The glyphs running down the left side and across the bottom are the names of towns in the province. Yautepec (third from the left in the bottom row) was part of Huaxtepec province. The people of Huaxtepec province paid the following goods in imperial taxes each year:

- 4 bins of food grains
- 4,000 gourd bowls
- 16,000 sheets of bark paper
- 8,000 cotton textiles of various types
- 46 fancy feathered warriors' costumes.

This is an impressive quantity of goods that required considerable effort by several thousand provincial households to produce and assemble, yet it was only one part of the total tax burden. Before Mexica conquest, people were already paying taxes to their local king, and the imperial taxes were simply added on top of these.

Comparing the impacts of city-states and the empire on the people of Morelos, several things are clear. First, people had far more voice in how things worked at the city-state level than at the imperial level, if only because of the facts of distance. No one lived very far from the king, and city-state decisions were made locally. Of course the same facts of distance meant that people found it harder to avoid

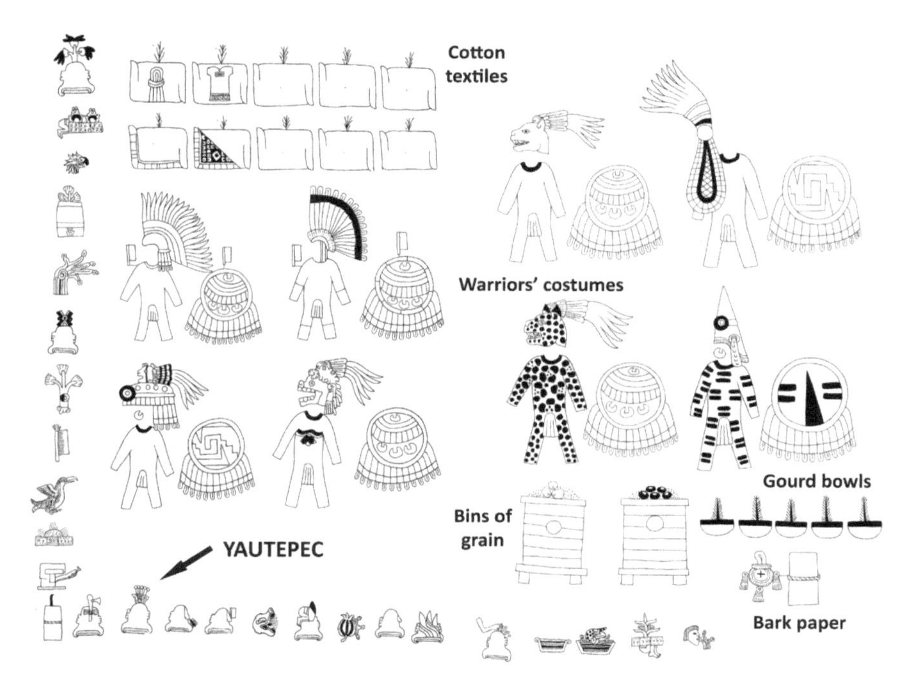

FIGURE 4.4 Imperial tax paid by Yautepec and other towns in the Huaxtepec province. From *The Codex Mendoza* (Berdan and Anawalt 1992: folio 24v, 25r); reproduced courtesy of Frances Berdan.

the king's agents when they went to round up people for a work gang. Second, in return for their taxes, people received far more services from their city-state than from the empire. Protection, in the form of restraint from re-conquering the area, was not much of a service. So why did people put up with the empire at all?

The Monty Python film *Life of Brian* provides some perspective. Set in the eastern Roman Empire, the head of a local rebel band defiantly asks his crew, "What have the Romans ever done for us?" To his dismay, they respond with a long list of services, including aqueducts, sanitation, roads, irrigation, education, public baths, wine and peace. The Roman Empire relied primarily on direct control, and these services were simply part of the deal. People paid taxes, and they got services in return, just as taxes translate into services in our governments today. But the Mexica and other empires organized with indirect control provided no such services in the provinces, so the question of why people put up with empires in these cases is harder to answer. But considering the nature of Aztec social classes and inequality will suggest a solution.

The 1 percent and the 99 percent

While we talk today about the gap between the super-wealthy one percent and the non-wealthy 99 percent, in Aztec times that discussion focused on nobles and commoners. Wealth inequality is present in nearly all societies, but it can take very different forms. Today there are few legal barriers to upward mobility, and sometimes people of modest means become millionaires. The Aztecs, on the other hand, had a system of social classes that allowed very limited upward mobility. If you were born a commoner, you stayed a commoner your whole life. You could accumulate wealth, but you could never enjoy the privileges of a noble.

While the commoners of Morelos received few if any benefits from the Mexica Empire, the story was very different for provincial nobles. They welcomed the opportunity to cooperate with Tenochtitlan's system of indirect rule because they profited from it. My excavations showed some of the privileges and advantages that nobles had over commoners—nobles lived in larger and fancier houses, and they had better access to valuable and imported goods. They benefitted from a pair of fundamental rights in Aztec society. First, nobles owned the land. Commoners had to pay nobles to use farmland, through rent or sharecropping. And second, nobles ran the city-state government. The king, of course, was a noble, but so too were all the top city-state officials.

When city-states were founded throughout central Mexico in the Settlement Period, nobles managed to gain control of the farmland. At first there were only a few noble families in any city-state, so young nobles had to search out other city-states to find spouses. Marriages across city-state lines became a form of diplomacy, and kings used this process to forge alliances.

Not only did nobles marry across city-state lines, but they also visited nobles in other city-states for official events such as royal weddings, funerals, and temple dedication ceremonies. The Spanish friars described some of these gatherings in Tenochtitlan, and they were elaborate festivals indeed. The lords exchanged expensive gifts—jewelry, feather art, and other items—and the host provided a sumptuous feast with the finest foods and alcoholic drinks. Music, dances, and plays were performed, orators gave speeches, and the festivals often culminated in theatrical ceremonies of human sacrifice. Various perks and privileges—from the right to drink hot chocolate to the benefits of literacy—helped nobles set themselves apart from commoners.

By the time the Mexica Empire was formed in 1428, the royal houses of different city-states were heavily inter-married, similar to the royal families of Europe. For example, the mother of one of the most powerful Mexica emperors, Motecuhzoma I, was a princess from Cuauhnahuac (Cuernavaca) in Morelos whose father was a powerful regional king (in fact, the people of Capilco and Cuexcomate were his subjects). As the empire expanded, the emperors found it easy to buy off provincial nobles. They made deals with local kings, many of them relatives by birth or marriage. The local rulers could stay in power so long as they paid the imperial taxes. Where did these funds come from? The conquered city-state kings simply increased the taxes on their local subjects and passed the imperial portion on to Tenochtitlan. City-state kings who cooperated were backed by the empire. I would guess that local kings may have increased taxes even beyond what the empire required, and kept the difference. Protected by the empire, they had a good thing going.

So why did people put up with the empire? Few services were provided, and few troops or administrators were posted in the provinces. Why go through the effort of producing thousands of extra cotton textiles, bowls, paper, and other goods for imperial taxes each year? The answer is that the local king and nobility supported the empire, and they made sure that people paid their imperial taxes. Commoners did not really have much choice. If they refused to pay taxes or rebelled in some way, they would be punished by their city-state government or by their landlord. This was one of the goals of the imperial rulers in Tenochtitlan: they could leave local control in local hands and the conquered city-states took the brunt of any discontent over taxes. If people complained to their local king, however, I'm sure he blamed the big bad empire for the heavy taxes.

Successful rural households

In spite of being exploited by nobles, kings, and the Mexica Empire, the households at Capilco and Cuexcomate managed to achieve a high quality of life. The contents of the middens behind each house signaled their prosperity. Although I had learned much from this project, the results opened up many questions. Were these the only well-off commoners in the Aztec provinces, or was prosperity more widespread? Was the slight decline in the quality of life under the Mexica Empire caused by local problems in the Buenavista hills (such as overpopulation), or was it caused by exploitation by the empire? To answer these and other questions, I needed information from household excavations at other sites. At the time (1990), no one else was doing this work, so Cindy and I packed up our gear and our girls and moved to Yautepec for a new round of excavations. The new setting differed from the Buenavista hills in two important ways: the Yautepec Valley had some of the richest farmland in central Mexico, and Aztec Yautepec was a city, not a village or town. But, against my expectations, I would find that the commoner households of Yautepec were remarkably similar to those at Capilco and Cuexcomate.

Notes

1 Frances Berdan was the leader of our summer seminar at Dumbarton Oaks, in both intellectual activities and volleyball. Other members were Richard Blanton, Elizabeth Boone, Mary Hodge, Emily Umberger, and myself.

2 Some of the major works by these authors are: Bowles and Gintis (2002), Ostrom (1990, 2009), and Sen (1992, 1999). Historian Daniel Curtis (2014) reaches similar conclusions about the resilience of some (but not all) rural communities in the face of exploitation by states and lords.

3 Scholars often use the term "tribute" to refer to Aztec taxes, but this is an incorrect label. As I explain in several articles (Smith 2014, 2015b), the Aztec system of state revenue fits the standard definition of tax (regular payments of set amounts, made according to the calendar, kept in written records, and administered by professional tax collectors). It does not fit the standard definition of tribute (a lump-sum payment made under duress).

5

EXCAVATIONS IN AN URBAN COMMUNITY

During the final lab season for Capilco and Cuexcomate, in 1989, a crew from the Morelos INAH office was excavating an Aztec mound at the edge of Yautepec, a city east of Cuernavaca. My graduate school advisor, David Grove, had shown me this mound many years earlier. Dave knew the archaeology of the state of Morelos like no one else, and we stopped to take a look at the Yautepec structure on one of our trips across the state. Covering 1.7 acres, it was the ruin of the largest ancient building in the entire state, and it must have been a palace or temple complex. When the landowner died, his heirs planned to sell the land for a housing subdivision, which would have meant destruction for the mound. A local organization, the Yautepec Cultural Society, petitioned INAH to excavate the structure and save it from being damaged or demolished. Cindy and I took a day off from lab work in Cuernavaca to visit the excavations, and we ended up spending several years digging at Yautepec ourselves.

The Yautepec mound turned out to be a big stone platform with stairs running up the west side (Figure 5.1). A series of rooms, passages, and courtyards covered the top of the platform. The construction quality was excellent (much better than Group 6 at Cuexcomate), with heavy use of plaster on the floors and walls, many of which were painted with colorful geometrical designs and religious symbols. Based on its architecture, the Yautepec platform must have been the royal palace for the king of Yautepec, one of the more powerful city-states in Morelos. An early Spanish map accompanying a land sale in Yautepec includes a sketch of the ruined platform as a reference point, and it is labeled *palacio*, or palace (Smith 2008: 115–119).

Hortensia de Vega Nova and other INAH archaeologists suggested that Cindy and I move our operation to Yautepec and excavate houses. A big area of vacant land next to the palace—the downtown area of a major Aztec city—was "protected"

FIGURE 5.1 Mexican excavations at the Yautepec royal palace in 1989. They are clearing off the front wall of the palace; the stairs led up into the living quarters. Photograph by Michael E. Smith.

as an official archaeological site. No one had excavated houses in the center of an Aztec city, and we were tempted. I hesitated, however, because I was in the process of trying to start a different project: a more intensive study of Aztec terracing in the Buenavista hills.

For a variety of reasons, however, that project fell through at just about the time I accepted a teaching position at the University at Albany (State University of New York). Albany has the best program in Mesoamerican anthropology of any U.S. university, including a good Ph.D. program (lacking at the smaller Loyola University). As a new professor I was expected to mount a fieldwork project quickly and take students into the field. These two developments tipped the scale in favor of a project at Yautepec, so I gave up on the terracing idea.

Capilco and Cuexcomate were small sites in a marginal environment, located far from the major Aztec capitals. I had been surprised to find their residents much wealthier and better connected to the outside world, and rural society far more complex, than anyone had suspected. Now Cindy and I were going to excavate a major capital city in one of the richest valleys of central Mexico. Were the people of Yautepec even richer than their country cousins? Did they have a more complicated and sophisticated urban society? Almost nothing was known about urban life in Aztec Mexico, apart from written sources on the imperial capital Tenochtitlan. If we could shed light on households and communities in Yautepec, this could help scholars better understand the variety of urban experiences around the world. Urbanization is advancing rapidly today, along with urban problems such as poverty, crime, environmental destruction, and loss of community. The more we know about the diversity of cities around the world throughout history, the easier it will be to find solutions for the urban challenges of today and tomorrow. As

Winston Churchill once said, "The farther back we look, the farther ahead we can see." Perhaps our archaeological study of Yautepec could contribute to knowledge on this larger scale.

The Yautepec Valley was a much more attractive area for the expanding Mexica Empire than the hilly terrain of the Buenavista Hills. It had more people to pay taxes and higher productivity. Did imperial conquest have a stronger effect in Yautepec, or was this community also resilient to conquest? I wanted to ask research questions similar to those we asked in western Morelos, but in a very different environmental and social context. This would lead to a better understanding of both the Mexica Empire and the local households and communities of Morelos. With these and other questions in mind, I obtained another grant from the National Science Foundation and another fieldwork permit from the Mexican authorities. Cindy and I packed up our girls and headed back to Mexico for fieldwork at Yautepec. Compared to our former trips from Chicago to Cuernavaca, however, the voyage from Albany, New York, added two days of driving.

Urban survey: knocking on doors and being chased by dogs

Our first season at Yautepec in the summer of 1985 was "urban archaeology" in both senses of the phrase: archaeological study of an ancient city, and archaeological fieldwork in the middle of a modern city (Smith et al. 1994). Aztec Yautepec had been a bustling capital city with thousands of residents, much larger than Capilco or Cuexcomate, and most of the site is buried under modern Yautepec. This made our first season radically different from the earlier project. Instead of mapping house foundations in a peaceful rural setting, we were looking for artifacts within a busy modern city.

Unlike at Capilco and Cuexcomate, artifacts on the ground surface were an important source of information at Yautepec. Archaeological sites—the houses, artifacts, and other traces of past activities—are typically buried over time by normal soil processes. Soil is created and builds up gradually from decomposing plants and other organic material, and soil gets moved from one place to another by erosion and human activity. At Capilco and Cuexcomate, the top soil layers had eroded away, which is why the house foundations were exposed. At Yautepec, on the other hand, the entire site had been buried—anywhere from one to three feet deep. Even at buried sites, artifacts often move up to the surface of the ground by agricultural plowing and disturbance from modern construction. Artifacts brought to the surface by plowing are usually a good guide to what lies buried, and archaeologists can learn quite a bit about sites just from the study of surface remains, without excavation.

My plan was to use surface artifacts at Yautepec to accomplish three goals. First, they would let us locate the borders of the Aztec city. The extent of the ancient occupation was not obvious, as it had been at the relatively undisturbed sites of Capilco and Cuexcomate. Second, I wanted to study the locations of ancient activities across the site, and surface artifacts have been used elsewhere for this purpose. And third, the surface collections would help identify places to excavate the following season. Unfortunately, we only managed to achieve the first goal.

The basic tool for archaeological survey is the aerial photograph. We marked up a government air photo of Yautepec with a grid of squares, each 100 by 100 meters (each square was one hectare in area; one hectare equals 1.5 acres). Cindy and I each led a survey crew with two graduate students and a local worker. We walked along the streets, through empty lots and across agricultural fields at the edge of town. In alternate squares on the map, we took a collection of surface artifacts. A student marked off a square of two by two meters, using stakes and string. We then collected all the artifacts within the square—mostly potsherds (Figure 5.2).

The open fields west of the palace, where we intended to excavate the following season, were full of artifacts, with stone wall foundations poking out into modern ditches. We started here and headed west along the grid lines until we could see few or no artifacts on the surface over a distance of 200 meters. We then drew the site boundary on the air photo, marking the edge of the area with abundant artifacts. Once we had located the western border of the site this way, the two crews worked their way gradually around the site going back and forth along the grid lines, filling out forms, taking collections, and marking the site boundary on the air photo. We covered almost six square kilometers that summer, and ended up with a map of Aztec Yautepec that covered just under two square kilometers (three-quarters of a square mile).

FIGURE 5.2 Field crew making a surface collection in a corn field at Yautepec.

Yautepec today straddles the Yautepec River in the midst of a wide floodplain of rich soils. The irrigation canals that today bring water to sugar cane, maize, and other crops had their origins in canals built by Aztec farmers to irrigate their maize and cotton fields. Our survey included everything from cultivated fields to vacant lots to built-up urban streets. The best conditions were in maize fields, where it is easy to see artifacts on the surface, particularly after a rainfall. The sugar cane fields that cover much of the Yautepec Valley today presented the worst survey conditions. Cane plants are densely packed with a poor view of the ground, and the edges of the long, thin leaves are sharp enough to slice one's skin like a paper cut. Anyone who has spent time in mature corn fields knows how the leaves have sharp edges, but sugar cane leaves do far more bodily damage. It was easy enough to take a surface collection at the edge of a cane field, but to look for surface artifacts within a field required pushing through the sharp leaves trying to avoid getting sliced up, and then having trouble seeing the ground surface at all. One of our workers took to wearing a baseball catcher's mask to protect his face when he had to go into a cane field.

Within the modern city we could see the ground surface best in the yards of houses. As in most Mexican cities, yards in Yautepec are walled or fenced. We spent a lot of time knocking on doors to ask people if we could look around in their yards. They were skeptical and hesitant, partly because this was a strange request from foreigners, and partly because they knew that all archaeological features belong to the Mexican government, whether on private or public land. By law, owners could be evicted and their property confiscated by eminent domain if we discovered important remains. Although this almost never happens in practice, it did make landowners reluctant to let us into their yards.

One episode where we tried to collect artifacts without the permission of the landowner shows why such permission is important. A large agricultural field at the edge of downtown Yautepec was surrounded by a wall. The owner's family operated a small store nearby, and I asked every day to enter the lot. "All we want to do is walk around the edge of the field and collect a few sherds." The women who ran the store always replied that only her husband could give permission, but he was never around. This lot was located at a critical place for our developing map of the boundaries of the Aztec-period town. After two weeks without progress, we hopped the wall and took a quick surface collection before anyone saw us. But just as we were closing up the last artifact bag, the women from the store showed up with a loaded shotgun. "Get out of here now. If I ever see you in this field again, you'll be sorry!" Needless to say, we obeyed her orders.

The dogs of Yautepec also slowed us down. Many dogs ran free, often in packs, and foreign archaeologists were good targets for barking and chasing. These small skinny street dogs were loud and brave when they were in a pack some distance away. We found, however, that bending down to pick up a rock from the ground, as if to throw it, was a signal the dogs understood.

Our survey efforts got some help from public service ads on the local radio station, Radio Campesino, urging people to cooperate with the foreign archaeologists.

These were sponsored by the Council to Support the Yautepec Archaeological Site, a local group that helped us in many ways. We discovered that female crew members who spoke good Spanish had the best luck gaining entry to people's yards. Our overall success rate was about one-half of the houses where we asked permission. In the most heavily built-up downtown area, we had to rely on construction trenches, unpaved alleys, and anyplace else where we could see the ground. The fact that the modern downtown was somewhat displaced from the Aztec downtown was a big help.

We faced some difficult conditions in Yautepec that summer. Radical political groups protested the government's efforts to turn control of the municipal water supply over to private hands. Political violence erupted and someone was killed. While it was not hard for us to steer clear of the water politics, it was harder to know what to do about an outbreak of cholera that swept through town during our survey. Cholera had recently arrived in Mexico through a traveler from Peru. The authorities said the outbreak was not serious, but local newspapers claimed the government was covering up the true extent of the disease. The main messages to the public were to take care with hygiene and avoid food prepared by street vendors.

We typically carried sandwiches from home and at lunchtime bought a soft drink and sat in the shade to eat. One day we were eating our sandwiches under a tree while a street vendor was preparing great-smelling fried tacos across the street. I could see that she didn't have running water to wash the utensils, so cholera was a worry.

"Boy, that sure smells good." I said after a few bites of a tasteless sandwich.

"Yeah, but what about cholera?" asked a student.

"That's not stopping a long line of customers," I replied. I couldn't stand it much longer and started to stand up.

Cindy piped up. "Mike, you should be careful. Please don't eat any of those tacos." I usually take Cindy's advice, but that day I followed my nose and crossed the street. The taco was great and I didn't get sick.

At the end of the survey, the crew finished classifying the artifacts and Cindy, the girls, and I returned to Albany. Back in Albany, during the fall semester we compared the numbers of artifacts in the surface collections to the site boundaries as identified in the field, and made some adjustments (Figure 5.3). The resulting map satisfied our first objective—defining the Aztec city's borders—but not the other two goals for our survey. I was hoping that the kinds of artifacts in our surface collections would allow us to reconstruct some of the spatial patterns at Aztec Yautepec, such as the locations of craft workshops, or zones of elite residences (this was the second goal). Surface collections at other Aztec sites such as Huexotla and Otumba had been successful this way (Brumfiel 1980; Charlton et al. 2000), but our data did not reveal any clear patterning. Looking back, it seems that our collection squares were simply too small to include enough artifacts and the amount of modern disturbance at Yautepec was too great. The lack of success on my third goal—finding places to excavate—was due to an entirely different reason. We finished the survey intending to concentrate our excavations in the open fields west of the palace, but when we returned in January, we were greeted by an unpleasant surprise.

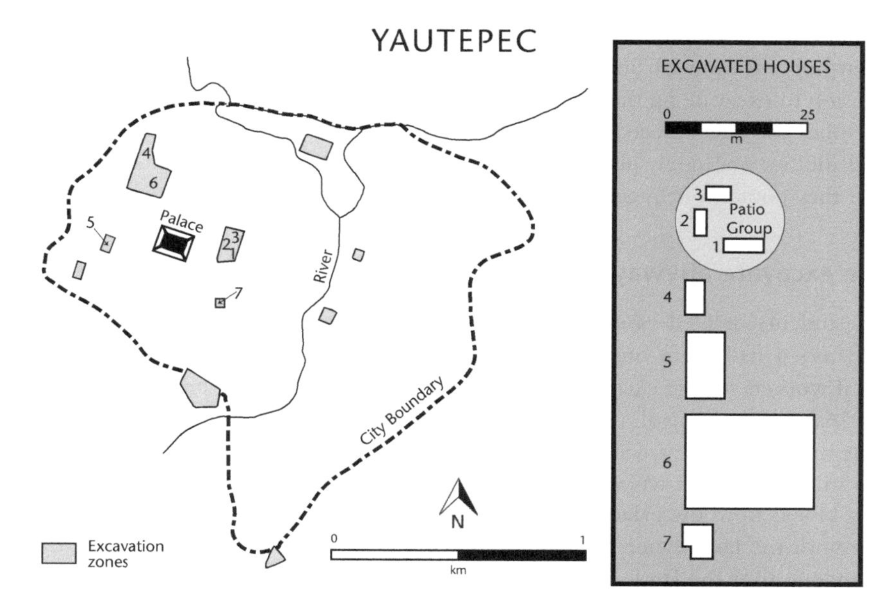

FIGURE 5.3 Map of Yautepec, showing the locations of excavation zones and the sizes of the houses we excavated. Map by Michael E. Smith, drawing by Shelby Manney.

The site is invaded by a squatters' settlement

We arrived in Yautepec in January of 1993 to find the fields where I had intended to excavate filled with tarpaper shacks. This squatters' settlement had sprung up literally overnight in September, the outcome of a well-planned land invasion. The Mexican term for the squatters, *paracaidistas*, means "parachutists." The parachutists claimed to be poor landless people who simply needed a place to live, and they immediately petitioned the authorities to install water, electricity, and other services in the new neighborhood. Other residents of Yautepec remarked that these squatters in fact all owned land elsewhere, and this was a land-grab to take advantage of the peculiarities of Mexican land-tenure laws. Illegal residents have far more rights than in the U.S. I later found out these invasions are a regular occurrence in Mexico (Ward 1978). The Yautepec invasion had a strong political component: city government was controlled by the long-standing dominant Mexican political party, the PRI, and the squatters were affiliated with an opposition party, the PRD.

The fact that the squatters occupied an official government archaeological zone gave this invasion more publicity than most. The city of Yautepec and INAH began legal proceedings to evict the squatters. Under the mistaken impression that this would be taken care of quickly, we went about getting ready to excavate. Cindy, the girls, and I moved back into the house we had rented before in Cuernavaca (a half-hour drive from Yautepec), and I rented a facility in Yautepec for the project. We were fortunate to get help from a prominent family of educators in Yautepec, the Peña Flores family. This family of teachers not only rented us the top floor of their house for our lab and student dormitory, but they also helped us secure permission to excavate on the grounds of two public schools in Yautepec. One family member was a co-director of the secondary school we worked in for two months, and another was highly placed in the education department of the State of Morelos. But they couldn't help get rid of the squatters.

We excavate anyway

As students arrived—most were graduate students and undergraduates from Albany—I had them organize our tools and equipment while I started to hire local workers for the excavations and the lab. For details of this project, see Smith (2016a) and Smith et al. (1999). When we were ready to start digging, it was clear that the squatters were not going to leave the site any time soon. In fact, they are still there today. My next choice of a place to excavate was a large open lot a few blocks from the palace with lots of potsherds on the surface. While negotiating with the landowner, I ran into one of the drawbacks of urban archaeology. Someone (not the landowner) told me that pesticides and fertilizers were stored in a barn on the property, and that toxic chemicals had been dumped around the lot in the past. Hazmat outfits were not included in my budget, so it was on to the third choice.

We started excavating in a large schoolyard of a secondary school located about a block from the palace. Two low mounds hinted at possible buried structures, and an ancient-looking stone wall was visible in one area. The schoolyard was littered with thousands and thousands of potsherds. Some of the New York students whose only archaeological experience had been on Iroquois sites were dumbfounded. The ground surface had more potsherds on it than the total number of sherds buried at many Iroquois sites. "Why hasn't someone picked these up?" they wanted to know. Aztec sites in general have lots of artifacts in them, just as most urban sites have more trash (that is, more artifacts) than the villages of tribal societies like the Iroquois. Yautepec would turn out to have especially abundant deposits, and a dense concentration of sherds on the ground surface was the norm. In fact, we excavated over one million potsherds on this project.

The assistant director of the school, María de la Concepción Peña Flores, was the landlord of our lab and she helped obtain permission to excavate. We started with all four crews looking for Aztec houses in different parts of the schoolyard. Cindy dug a trench in an area with the highest surface concentrations of artifacts. Although she did not find a house, she did hit a very rich midden with an excellent stratigraphic sequence of the three Aztec time periods (Settlement, Growth, and Imperial), one on top of another. This deposit helped us define a chronology for Yautepec that paralleled the three periods in the Buenavista hills. Someone in the Settlement Period had dug a big trash pit, and then people kept tossing things in for the next four centuries. My graduate student Lisa Montiel followed out a low stone wall, which turned out to be our first Aztec house at Yautepec, labeled House 4.

This structure consisted of a low platform (about one foot high) that served as the floor for a house made of adobe bricks. The other excavators worked in different parts of the schoolyard.

Working in the walled schoolyard had the advantage of protecting the excavations from damage by the people and animals of Yautepec, deliberate or not. The crews, however, were constantly under the gaze of hundreds of students in grades six through eight. I worked out an arrangement with the school to keep students away from the excavations, and in the afternoons teachers could bring classes out and we would explain what we were finding. Such educational outreach work is important in archaeology. The entire city of Yautepec is a big archaeological site, and over the long term it is the residents themselves who will either preserve or destroy the record of their Aztec ancestors. For this reason, the many hours we all talked to school classes and local residents were worth it.

As soon as the crews were under way in the schoolyard, I began looking for other places to excavate. This involved another round of knocking on doors and often lengthy negotiations with landowners. When I would gain access to a property, we would excavate a series of test pits—often in a checkerboard pattern—searching for a house or other Aztec deposit. The owner of a lot immediately next to the squatters' settlement wanted to build a house. He erected a high wall around his property to keep the squatters out and then informed INAH of his intentions. Normally it is INAH's responsibility to investigate such situations, often by conducting an excavation to recover any information prior to construction. But since we were already working in Yautepec, INAH turned to me, and I asked Susan Norris and her crew to start digging test pits.

Sue was a talented archaeologist who had just graduated from Albany. I had supervised her undergraduate research on Mesoamerican obsidian. During the excavation season Sue got acceptance letters from some of the best archaeology graduate programs. She turned down an offer from Arizona State University to attend Harvard. She would later return to our Yautepec lab for her PhD research on the local obsidian industry. Sue's test pits succeeded in locating a house, which turned out to be half-preserved. One side had been well buried and protected from plowing, while the other side had a shallower covering, and plowing had destroyed that portion of the house.

While Sue was working on this structure (House 5), the squatters were busy protesting at the state capital and denouncing our crew as foreign invaders. A group jumped over the wall into the lot and threatened Sue and her six workers. They said that if the local crew kept working for the gringos, they would get beaten up. One worker ran to complain to the offices of the dominant political party, and word eventually reached the governor of Morelos, who sent the state police to guard us. These were muscular, tough-looking guys in sunglasses and bright blue uniforms who carried shotguns. After they stood around bored for a few days, I suggested that perhaps they would like to help. I put them to work screening the dirt, which they found much more interesting than their normal guard duties (Figure 5.4).

FIGURE 5.4 State police officer excavating. Photograph by Michael E. Smith.

We had no further problems with the squatters, apart from the reporters who swarmed over Yautepec to cover the story. Attempts by the city to evict the squatters were unsuccessful. Our plight was featured on the Mexican weekly television news show, *Sesenta Minutos* (60 Minutes). I had some tricky interviews. It was easy to answer questions such as: were the squatters living on the archaeological site? (yes), were they damaging the archaeological remains? (yes), and were these important remains? (yes). But should the governor evict them forcibly? I had to bite my tongue here and answer, "No comment." I managed to avoid headlines like, "Foreign archaeologist Smith says people should be thrown out of their homes."

In the end I wasn't the one to give the most articulate account of the effects of the squatters on the Yautepec archaeological site. On alternate Fridays we hosted fifth-grade classes from local schools. We showed the students what we were doing and let them handle the artifacts as they came out of the ground (Figure 5.5). In the process, they learned about archaeology and about the history of their city. One Friday, a television news crew showed up during one of these sessions. A reporter asked one little girl what she had learned. Without any coaching at all, she launched into an eloquent speech that I remember like this:

> My ancestors built a great city here in Yautepec. These archaeologists came all the way from the United States to uncover this ancient city. They are discovering the great things our ancestors did, and they are teaching us about their finds. But now the squatters have built their shacks on top of the archaeological site. They are destroying the remains of my ancestors, and they are destroying the history of our city. This is not right!

FIGURE 5.5 Lecture and demonstration to a class of fifth graders. Photograph by Cynthia Heath-Smith; reproduced with permission.

When the camera panned over to me, I had to hide my delight at those remarks. But regardless of the law, and regardless of the sentiments of many residents of Yautepec—as articulated by this young student—the squatters remained on the site, and today their houses are more solid and the area is just another neighborhood of the city.

Up until this point, the urban households of Yautepec seemed remarkably similar to the rural households at Capilco and Cuexcomate. The houses were small structures, and the middens had the same kinds of artifacts. But our next excavation uncovered evidence for obsidian workshops, something not present at the other sites. I wanted to excavate in a big vacant lot behind the Yautepec municipal cemetery. It was not far from the palace, and had lots of artifacts on the surface. The owner was one of the wealthiest men in town. Among his many activities, he raised fighting bulls. Luckily, he kept the bulls elsewhere, not on this lot. My friends in Yautepec all seemed afraid of this person, and they spent days discussing the best way to approach him. I got fed up and just went up to him on the street one day, to the horror of one of my friends who had pointed him out. I started to explain who I was, but he stopped me before I could finish.

"Yes," he said, "I know you are the archaeologist, and you have been looking around my vacant lot. Please feel free to excavate there." So I did not have to go through the husband of the cousin of the friend to deal with this landowner. He also told me that his son was studying archaeology in college!

Lisa Montiel got started excavating in the lot behind the cemetery. Lisa had studied archaeology as an undergraduate at the University of Illinois, where my former advisor, Dave Grove, had turned her on to Mexican archaeology. She proved to be an excellent excavator, and went on to co-direct a regional survey of the Yautepec Valley with my other graduate student, Timothy Hare. They each wrote PhD dissertations on the survey project. Lisa put in a grid or checkerboard of test pits in the empty lot, and located three Aztec houses (Houses 1 to 3) arranged around an open area—the only intact patio group we found at Yautepec. The middens behind two of these contained significant numbers of waste flakes from the production of obsidian tools. House 3 had the only midden dating to the Spanish colonial period. This structure was built and used in the Imperial Period, and then continued in occupation through the first century or so of the Spanish Period. The midden from the latter period contained the same kinds of pottery and obsidian as the Aztec middens, but with the addition of cow and horse bones, iron nails, and glazed pottery, all traits introduced after the Spanish conquest.

As the excavations settled into a routine, the presence of foreign archaeologists became less remarkable to the people of Yautepec. My students developed friendships with local residents, and two female U.S. archaeologists (Lisa Montiel and Courtney Brown, an undergraduate who joined us during the summer) even married men from Yautepec. But while our interactions with Yautepec residents were almost always positive and friendly, we did not develop close friendships with our workers as we had when excavating at Capilco and Cuexcomate. Perhaps this was because we were working in a city of 40,000 residents, whereas Tetlama was a village of fewer than 1,000 people. Tetlama was a single community, and we were accepted into that community by our workers and their families. The social atmosphere in Yautepec, by contrast, was pervaded by politics. The standoff over the squatters occupying the archaeological zone was fueled by competition between political parties, and the local group that helped us hire workers tried to use political party affiliation as a criterion of employment (something I had to fight against).

Cindy and I also found that fewer of our crew seemed to be as talented and motivated as our workers from Tetlama. We did have some smart and dedicated workers in Yautepec, but these were fewer than in our earlier crew. Some of these urbanites had less farming experience (very relevant to excavation), but I think the main reason was the social atmosphere in the community. Yautepec was larger, far more politicized and less socially cohesive than Tetlama, and this affected the quality of the workers I could find. In this, as in so many ways, the nature of local communities makes a big difference.

Each day Cindy or I had to leave early to pick up our daughters from school in Cuernavaca. When summer came we continued excavating. School was out, and April and Heather would spend their days in Yautepec. We had some concerns for their safety, since kidnapping the children of rich families was not uncommon around Yautepec, where wealthy Mexico City families often spent their weekends. Many Mexicans think that gringos are wealthy, so we kept close tabs on our daughters. Much later, while finishing up this book, I read a newspaper story about how Yautepec is now the kidnapping capital of Mexico, with many of the victims killed or injured.

The archaeologists often ate at a small restaurant near the lab whose quesadillas were the best in town. The owner-chef had four young granddaughters who helped out. The students started calling this the "Little Girl Café" and April and Heather made friends with the four girls. All six girls attended a local day camp together, and I would drive them to camp and back each day in the project pickup truck. One day I got so involved in an excavation that I forgot to pick them up from camp. To get home they had to take the bus back to the lab. This was not a big deal to their Mexican friends, but we had forbidden our daughters to take buses because of our worries about security. The bus trip was a minor adventure for them, but years later they still kid me about the time I forgot to pick them up from camp.

Early in the field season, the director of public works for the city of Yautepec started to harass the field crews. He avoided me, but he told two of the female students it was illegal for them to be excavating in Yautepec. Anyone digging in the ground inside the city supposedly needed his permission, and we would all be in big trouble if we didn't stop. I checked with the city government and with INAH, and they assured me that I had full legal permission for our project. The public works department was run by the opposition political party, and this was just local politics as usual. I was naturally suspicious two months later when the same guy came into the lab and greeted me with a big hug like we were old friends (we had never actually met). While grading a dirt street, one of his crews uncovered a white pavement. They got into an argument about whether this was a modern cement pavement or an Aztec plaster floor, and he wanted me to resolve the question by excavating the feature (it looked to me like an Aztec house floor). Could this be a trap? Perhaps there really was a law that forbade excavating in a street and I would end up in jail.

After some assurances, I went ahead and put a crew on this feature, which turned out to be the plaster floor of a large Aztec house (House 7). Because the excavation was literally in the road—and extending into a small empty lot—there was no way to secure the area at night. I considered hiring a guard, but we were nearing the end of the field season, funds were running low, and I did not want to divert any workers away from the excavation for guard duty. But my fears were unfounded; the only disturbance was the smelly gift left by a local dog on the plaster floor each night (Figure 5.6). And I did not end up in jail for digging in the street.

An elite residence

Ever since we had started in the schoolyard, I had my eye on a large but low mound next to the basketball court, hoping it might be a preserved elite residence. Cuexcomate was still the only Aztec site where elite and commoner middens could be directly compared. The Yautepec royal palace was an elite residence of another order, but unfortunately the INAH archaeologists did not target possible middens next to the palace. As followers of the monumental archaeology approach, they focused on architecture, not trash. Perhaps the low mound in the schoolyard would turn out to be the residence of a non-royal noble family. My plan was to save this structure for our last excavation, but then some seventh-grade boys started digging into the mound with sticks, sending dirt flying all over the school's basketball court. They had seen our trenches, and decided that excavation was too much

FIGURE 5.6 House 7 at Yautepec, with a local dog. Photograph by Michael E. Smith.

fun to be left to the archaeologists. I quickly put an end to their destruction, but the boys did manage to uncover a plaster floor. When the basketball court had been built, the construction workers had to cut into one side of the mound to create a level surface. Through time, eroding soil and grass had covered up the exposed floor—until the pupils started their illicit excavation.

As I had found at Cuexcomate, digging a large elite residence (Structure 6) was far more complicated and time-consuming than excavating small commoner houses so I set my best archaeologist to work. Not only did Cindy have more field-work experience than the students, but she was particularly careful and systematic in her excavating and note-taking. There are few things as important in an excavation as good field notes, and on each of my projects I would have Cindy give lessons to the students on note-taking. Her meticulous notes, however, sometimes led to conflicts with me.

"Can't you move this excavation along a little faster?"

"But you are always telling us, Mike, that excavation is destruction, and without careful work and good notes we will lose important information."

"Yes, yes, I know. But I'd really like to get this trench done by the end of the week."

"Okay, then maybe you should be the one to pick up the girls in Cuernavaca today and tomorrow."

There was not time to clear the entire structure, which measured more than 4,000 square feet, so we excavated a pair of trenches at right angles across the mound. We learned three things about this building. First, the quality of construction was higher than any of the commoner houses in Yautepec, higher than the elite house at Cuexcomate. Though the construction materials and methods were not as fine as those at the royal palace, all of the walls and floors were covered with lime plaster, and many walls were built with squared-off stones. The building also had a complex history of expansion and remodeling over the centuries: walls were moved, new floors laid, and the overall configuration shifted several times. And modern construction activity had sheared off the southern and western sides of the building, making it difficult to estimate its total extent.

The intact outer walls on the north and east sides, however, were vitally important because they showed us where to look for trash deposits next to the structure. We extended our trenches beyond the building proper on those sides and were rewarded by rich stratified middens. Commoners and rural elites were not the only ones to toss their trash out back, and I thank the members of this urban elite family for doing the same thing. As at Cuexcomate, we noticed during excavation that the artifacts from the elite middens seemed to resemble those from commoner houses. But we wondered whether there would be differences between the types of houses in the quantities of key artifacts. The answer had to await our laboratory analyses. Although we got started classifying ceramics while still excavating, it took several summers of lab work before we had made much progress.

I stopped in a corner grocery store for a cold soft drink one day while driving between excavations. The owner asked whether the rumors were true that we had found buried pyramids in the schoolyard that would require the school to be torn down to continue the excavations. I assured him that while we had found buried buildings, none of them were pyramids and no one was going to tear down the school. In the public's mind, archaeologists excavate pyramids and look for treasure. The royal palace, a site open to the public, is known locally as "the pyramid." I explained to local residents many times that we were not looking for pyramids, but that message did not always sink in. Public education was a continuous process at Yautepec, and this influenced the fate of the excavated walls and floors of Structure 6.

Excavation of Structure 6 took until the end of the field season in July. Although I was instructed to rebury most of the houses we had uncovered, officials from INAH asked me to keep this excavation open. A crew from INAH took over and cleared the rest of the structure. They consolidated the architecture to withstand the rain and elements and left the excavation intact as an open-air museum in the schoolyard. Everyone thought this was a great idea, and many students got to see the building over the next few years. But the school's custodial staff did not have the training to maintain the ruin, and it proved impossible to keep students from climbing around and damaging the floors and walls (maybe those same kids with their sticks). The structure was deteriorating, so INAH ordered it reburied to preserve what was left.

Burial of the dead

Several of the schoolyard excavations turned up human burials. As at Capilco and Cuexcomate, most burials were located next to houses. Also like those sites, the burials we found were only a very small proportion of the numbers of people who had lived and died in Aztec Yautepec. Most of the burials were fairly normal examples of what archaeologists call primary burials. A primary burial is when a body is put in the ground shortly after death and the remains are undisturbed. When archaeologists excavate a primary burial, the bones are usually articulated, meaning that they are arranged in their correct anatomical relationship. Burial 11, for example, is a primary burial of three commoners—two adult males and an adolescent female—all placed in flexed positions up against the wall of House 4 (Figure 5.7).

Burial 3 contained two adult males whose bodies had been folded up, as if grasping their knees; archaeologists call this a flexed position. One of them had a four-inch long obsidian arrow-point embedded in a vertebra. This was surely the cause of death of this young man, but the burial site told us nothing of the context of his death. Perhaps he was a soldier, killed defending Yautepec against the Mexica imperial army, or maybe he was in the wrong place at the wrong time and killed by a jealous husband; we will never know. One of the excavations in

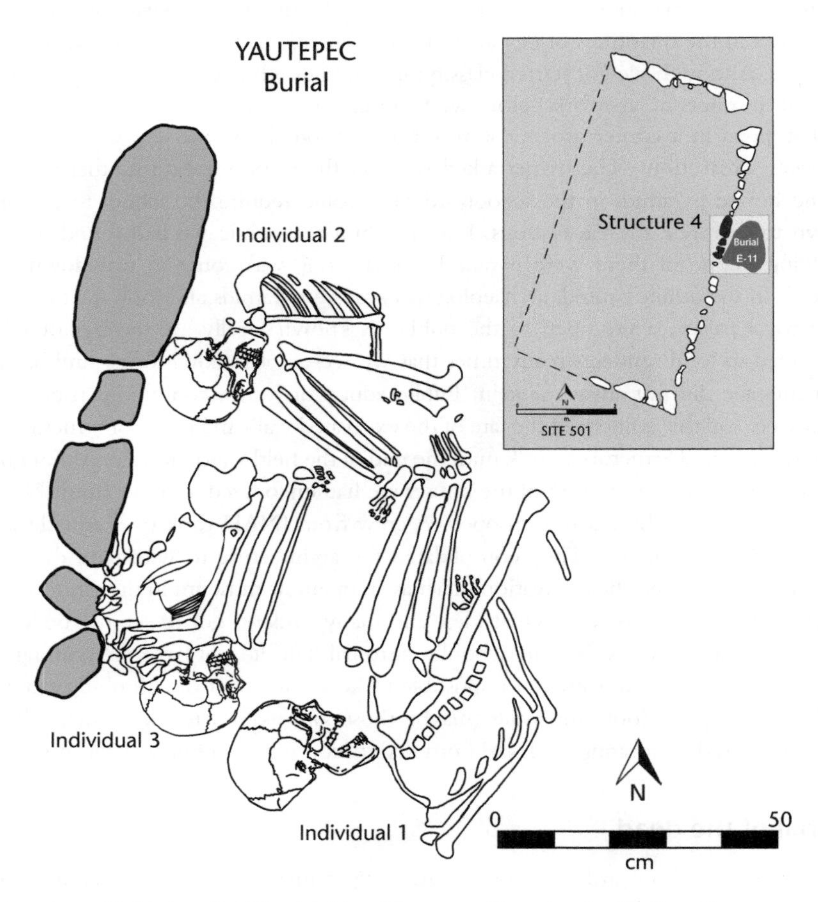

FIGURE 5.7 Field sketch of Burial 11 at Yautepec. Drawing by Shelby Manney.

the schoolyard uncovered a burial area for infants without any obvious building nearby. Within a small space, we found nine burials of late fetal or neonatal infants, several placed inside pottery bowls.

The most complicated of the Yautepec burials was Burial 2, located on the east side of House 4. This burial contains the remains of what I first thought was a sacrificial offering because of the way the skeletons were arranged—or, rather, scattered. The excavation of a burial is a painstaking and time-consuming process, even for regular primary burials. The bones have to be carefully cleared off, usually with dental picks and paintbrushes, and then each bone is drawn to scale and photographed. Finally, the bones are removed, taking care to label each one for later analysis by an osteologist, a specialist in the human skeleton.

Burial 2 looked like a complicated mess when Lisa Montiel first encountered the bones next to House 4. Three skulls suggested the presence of three people, but the bones appeared to be all mixed up. After the bones in the top layer were drawn and photographed Lisa removed them, revealing a single articulated skeleton underneath. This was the remains of an adult woman, buried with a ceramic bowl and a spindle whorl as offerings. The bones above this body were secondary burials—the skeletons were not fully articulated—of an adult male and a young adult female.

The unusual thing about the upper two individuals is that their bones were partially articulated. There was a pile of arm bones, two vertebral columns with articulated ribs, and two sets of articulated leg bones. The two skulls sat next to one another, but neither was articulated with a vertebral column. It looked like the bodies had been cut into large pieces—arms, legs, trunk, and head—before they were buried. I knew from historical sources that important Aztec nobles in Tenochtitlan were sometimes buried along with the sacrificed remains of servants, and at first Burial 2 looked like the possible remains of such a practice. Two facts, however, argued against this interpretation. For one thing, this burial was associated with House 4, clearly the residence of commoners, not nobles. But a bigger problem was that the bones showed no evidence of cut marks.

Cut marks on bone provide some of the best direct evidence for ancient human sacrifices. Osteologists have found many examples of cut marks—the traces of ancient knives—on ancient disarticulated skeletons all over the world. Cut marks are found on Aztec sacrificial burials excavated in Mexico City, and I assumed we would find them on the upper skeletons in Burial 2. Our osteologist, my University at Albany colleague Dr. Richard Wilkinson, was an expert on cut marks. But after careful study, he could find no such traces at all on the bones in Burial 2.

The lack of cut marks almost certainly ruled out human sacrifice for Burial 2, leaving the possibility that this was simply a secondary burial. Secondary burials result when the body is left to partially or fully decay in a temporary location, and then the remains are gathered up and given a formal burial in a grave or tomb. This practice was common in ancient cultures around the world, including Mesoamerica. For Burial 2, a likely scenario runs as follows. Two individuals (probably from the family living in Structure 4) died and their bodies were given the first stage of a secondary burial. They would have been buried in a marked location. Then, after some time had passed, the third individual died (the articulated female with the grave offerings), and the other two bodies were dug up so that they could be reburied with her. Perhaps the three were relatives, and their family wanted them to be in the same grave. The two bodies from the secondary burial must have been only partially decomposed, and they either fell apart into sections or were separated, perhaps to fit better in the small grave pit. I admit that this interpretation is speculative, but it does fit the facts of Burial 2.

We excavated one other human bone that signals some kind of processing of the body after death: a notched or grooved femur (thigh bone). The Aztecs sometimes removed the femur from a body after death because of its religious symbolism. These bones stood for continuity and fertility. Friar Sahagún and the chroniclers tell us that the femur was sometimes hung from a tree for display outside the house. In other cases the bone was cut with deep parallel grooves to make a kind of rasp or musical instrument for use in ceremonies. These grooved femurs were very common in the western part of the Mexica Empire, often reburied with offerings as secondary burials. At Yautepec, Cindy had her workers sift through the backdirt from a modern construction project, where they found a segment of a grooved femur. Without good excavated context, however, we don't know which period this is from, or whether it was from a burial, a midden, or some other deposit.

We did end up with one likely case of human sacrifice, but without a good context—we can't even be sure it was from Yautepec. While Lisa Montiel was excavating Houses 1, 2 and 3, the landowner—the one with the fighting bulls—began construction of a driveway in another part of the property. His workers were excavating a trench to lay a drainage pipe, and we periodically checked to see if they had found any archaeological remains. One day, one of them came over to our excavations with a gift: a set of two deep nested bowls that contained a human skull, embedded in dried soil. He claimed to have removed this from the trench he was digging, but I took a look and could see no other remains near the place where the bowls had supposedly been found. I expected to see traces of a house of other building nearby, or perhaps other offerings. It is equally likely that the guy had found the bowls elsewhere (in Yautepec, or even in another town) and wanted to give them to the archaeologists without letting on where he got them. Nobody in Mexico wants archaeologists to find out that their land has a site on it.

In any case, I accepted the gift, cataloged it as Burial 20, and brought it back to the lab to excavate the skull from the bowls. The lab crew (several undergraduates) spent most of their time cataloging artifacts and supervising sherd washing, and they were glad to have something more interesting to do. They got out the dental picks and used all the care we normally give to a burial to carefully remove the skull from the packed soil of the bowls. They found evidence that the head had been cut off while the body was fresh and intact: one of the cervical or neck vertebrae was articulated with the skull in the bottom of the bowl. When a skull is removed from a secondary burial, where it had naturally fallen away from the neck bones, it does not have the neck vertebrae still attached. But when someone is beheaded the skull is always articulated with one or two vertebrae. Because we have no good contextual information on this find—it was not even necessarily from Yautepec—it is impossible to judge its significance or meaning. While this is an interesting find, it furnishes no solid evidence about life in Aztec Yautepec. All that's certain is that somewhere, at some point in the Aztec past, somebody was beheaded.

Although I found no definitive evidence for human sacrificial practices in domestic settings, the lack of context for some of these items is frustrating and leaves the situation murkier than I'd like. But a different kind of evidence from Wilkinson's skeletal analyses is much clearer: these were healthy people. He noted that the adult bones from Yautepec showed very low levels of disease and pathology and high levels of indicators of dietary quality. Childhood malnutrition—not uncommon in the distant past—leaves some characteristic markings on the bone, and our skeletons lacked these. In fact, he remarked these were among the healthiest individuals whose bones he had ever studied (Wilkinson 1998). Since in ancient times an individual's level of health typically reflected the wealth of his or her household, the bones support the idea that the households of Yautepec were economically well-off. Like the people of Capilco and Cuexcomate, the urbanites of Yautepec had a high quality of life.

Irrigation and urban agriculture

While the people of Capilco and Cuexcomate relied on terracing to grow crops, the major type of intensive agriculture at Yautepec was canal irrigation. But unlike the terraces, which survived for us to map and excavate, we could infer the Yautepec irrigation system only from indirect evidence. The floodplain of the Yautepec River has deep, fertile soils that are heavily irrigated today, and much of the modern irrigation system uses the same simple technology that was available to the Aztecs (Figure 5.8). Written records report that the Spaniards found the valley covered with irrigated fields of cotton and maize. The new overlords took over the Aztec irrigation system and replaced cotton and maize with sugar cane, one of the top commodities in world trade at the time.

We excavated a line of test pits across an irrigated field to look for houses or middens. If I was correct in assuming that it had been irrigated in Aztec times, we might find a few artifacts but no traces of houses or middens, and this is precisely what we found. Our uppermost trench in the line was placed immediately next to the modern irrigation canal running along the edge of the field. I was hoping that the course of the canal might have been moved since the Aztec period, leaving the Aztec canal intact for us to find, but this was not to be. Most likely the modern canal follows the same channel as the ancient canal.

Excavation in the churchyard

Because of its agricultural riches, Yautepec was one of the first cities in Morelos to be settled by Spaniards. Two churches were built in the sixteenth century.

FIGURE 5.8 Irrigation dam and men cleaning out a canal. Drawing by Kagan McLeod.

The main church and monastery complex rose in 1548, and a smaller neighborhood church appeared across the river, probably soon thereafter. The Spaniards usually tore down the main pyramid of an Aztec city and built a church on top of the rubble. They did this to make a symbolic statement to the native peoples: behold a new Christian God who is more powerful than the old pagan deities—you must convert to Christianity. Was there an Aztec temple under the church?

I wanted to excavate close to The Assumption of Our Lady of Yautepec, the main church in Yautepec. Built in 1548, it is still an active Catholic parish church. Next to the church stands a cloister where monks had once lived. The *capilla abierta*, or open chapel, also survives. In these early churches, the open chapel was like the stage of a theater—a raised platform built into a stone structure, with one side open to the churchyard. It was always the first structure to be built. The friars preached to the natives here while the main church and monastery were being constructed. I obtained permission from the priest in charge to conduct some test excavations in the atrium (the walled churchyard) and the open chapel. The only thing these excavations turned up were burials from the historical period, long after the Spanish conquest. Churchyards (and evidently open chapels) were used as cemeteries back then, typically without marked graves. We found no intact Aztec deposits at all. I have no idea why the Spaniards in Yautepec built their church on a new site instead of over an Aztec temple, or why they laid out their city at some distance from the church.

We also placed some test pits in the atrium of the small church in the neighborhood called San Juan. Sue Norris excavated several test pits and found very deep deposits of river alluvium, but without Aztec remains. In fact, one excavation turned up some pots from the Epiclassic Period (AD 700–900) buried under about six feet of alluvial soil. This reveals several episodes of major flooding of the Yautepec River between the Epiclassic and Spanish Periods.

Each of the sixteenth-century churches made use of an Aztec stone box as a vessel for holy water (Figure 5.9). These square boxes of basalt originally held human hearts after a sacrifice ritual. The box was closed with a stone lid, and the heart carefully guarded for its supernatural power. In the main church, an Aztec stone box is built into a pillar in the cloister, and in the San Juan chapel the box is part of the exterior front wall. I often wonder whether the early friars and their native builders knew they were using sacrificial cult objects for their water basins. Were these just convenient receptacles for holy water, or was this another deliberate Christian use of an Aztec religious item to advertise the dominance of the new religion over the old?

FIGURE 5.9 Aztec stone box embedded in the wall of the sixteenth-century Catholic convent of the Dominican Order in Yautepec. Photograph by Michael E. Smith.

It would not be surprising if the kings and priests of Aztec Yautepec carried out human sacrifices, as their peers did in most Aztec cities. They probably used these stone boxes in their rituals, and later the boxes ended up in the hands of the friars. But my story is less about these Aztec leaders than about their commoner subjects. None of the excavations turned up evidence for sacrificial rituals in residential contexts. Human sacrifice was part of Aztec state religion, a domain far removed from the lives of most Aztec people. To understand those lives at Yautepec, we now need to look at the artifacts.

6

URBAN LIFE

The opposition between rural and urban has been a major theme in Western thought for thousands of years. As soon as the first cities were established—during the Urban Revolution 5,000 years ago—writers began praising the virtues of cities over the countryside. To the ancient Sumerians, life was ordered and safe in the city, while wild beasts and outlaws prowled the countryside. To the Romans, the city was the home of civic virtue. In recent centuries, however, these judgments were reversed: the countryside is seen as the source of positive values, which are corrupted by the city. Even if we ignore the value judgments, we are left with the widespread notion that the city and the country are very different places. This perspective has become enshrined in both urban scholarship and the popular imagination to the point where it seems right and appropriate: life in the city is unlike life in the countryside.

Over several seasons, however, our laboratory studies gradually revealed that the people of Yautepec led lives almost identical to those of their rural cousins. The houses were the same size and built of the same materials, and people used the same kinds of things in their daily lives. They had similar access to foreign imports and styles. My expectations, based on the idea that rural and urban life must be very different, were mistaken. The wealth and connections of the rural households had made them seem "urban-like," and now the urban households—people living in small adobe houses with modest artifacts—seemed "rural-like." It turns out that rural and urban were just not all that different in Aztec-period Morelos.

Daily life

Nearly all of the artifacts from the Yautepec middens were very similar to those from Cuexcomate and Capilco, the ones I described in Chapter 3. All of the households had tortilla griddles and stone grinding tools. The people of Yautepec used thinner *comales* to bake their tortillas, but their *manos* and *metates* were no different than those owned by their rural cousins. Everyone had access to obsidian. The Yautepec households had more obsidian than their country cousins and the quantitative patterns of imports were slightly different, but the obsidian blade was still the basic cutting tool of choice in both regions. Spindle whorls and spinning bowls were abundant in all of the Yautepec middens, just as they had been at the rural sites. People used incense burners and figurines for domestic rituals, and most had musical instruments. The long-handled censer was the ritual item of choice in both regions, but the people of Yautepec added a second type of censer to burn their incense. Most ceramic figurines conformed to the basic Aztec central Mexican figurine style, but while one local style was used at Capilco and Cuexcomate, two different local styles were common at Yautepec. If we could see into the ancient houses, the interiors in the two areas would have been quite similar. In fact, they both would have resembled the interior of a modern peasant house in one of the remote parts of central Mexico where an indigenous language is still spoken (Figure 6.1).

FIGURE 6.1 Interior of a kitchen. Drawing by Kagan McLeod.

We found fragments of a special kind of cup—a polished red goblet—that was used to drink hot chocolate (Figure 6.2). These had not been present at Capilco and Cuexcomate. Aztec paintings show nobles consuming a chocolate drink from fancy red goblets that resemble a modern brandy snifter in shape. Cacao beans would have been used as money at both Yautepec and the rural sites. It seems logical to assume that drinking hot chocolate was something only the well-off would do. Most archaeologists had assumed that only Aztec nobles consumed the drink, but sherds from these chocolate goblets came from commoner middens at Yautepec as well as the elite middens. The cacao vessels furnish one of the few indications that the commoners of Yautepec may have been wealthier than the peasants of Capilco and Cuexcomate.

Our laboratory in Yautepec

Our laboratory was set up on the upper floor of the residence of the Peña Flores family in Yautepec. While not as picturesque or historically interesting as my previous lab in Maximilian's old stable in Cuernavaca, the Yautepec lab had some advantages. Because it was located in town, it was much easier to travel between lab and field during the excavations. The lab consisted of two storage rooms plus a large open patio, the roof of the main residence below. We fixed up some awnings and set up our tables (Figure 6.3). Natural light is best for studying artifacts, and we could expand or contract our work area as needed. The large flat patio area gave us

FIGURE 6.2 Goblet for drinking cacao, from an offering at the nearby site of Coatetelco. Photograph by Michael E. Smith.

FIGURE 6.3 Students and local workers sorting sherds in our Yautepec lab. Photograph by Michael E. Smith.

space to lay out clean artifacts to dry, and we had no trouble filling it up most days during the excavations. Over one million potsherds were dried on this patio. The family rented rooms to the students, and I paid to install a new bathroom.

While having the lab close to the excavations certainly had its advantages, the daily need for Cindy or me to leave Yautepec early to pick up the girls from school in Cuernavaca was not very convenient. Whoever was on duty would bring the girls home and get them started on their homework. Morning classes at their school were offered in Spanish, while afternoon classes were taught in English. After homework in both languages, the girls could play with friends in the neighborhood.

April and Heather both went through a period of near-constant intestinal ailments, from simple diarrhea to amoebic dysentery. We got to know the pediatrician in our neighborhood quite well. I recall carrying Heather down the street to the doctor because she was too sick and dehydrated to walk. We always boiled our drinking water and we would lecture the girls about clean water and contamination. Boiling water was a big deal in our household routine, taking up hours of stove time every day. We used boiled water for cooking, we washed fresh vegetables in boiled water, and we insisted the girls brush their teeth with boiled water. Many years later, after they were grown up, April and Heather made a confession.

"We used to drink water from the garden hose with our friends." Well, that explained the intestinal problems! Cindy and I were dumbfounded.

"But why did you do that?"

"Because we weren't supposed to."

I hired local women to wash the artifacts. Many of these were wives or sisters of the men working on the excavations. With an average of 10,000 sherds arriving in the lab each day, the bags of unwashed pottery quickly built up. Several times I had to hire additional people to wash. After a while, I chose the smartest and most observant of the women to learn the ceramic classification. At the end of the excavations I picked the best of these workers and the smartest excavation workers to be our long-term lab crew. They worked for the project every summer, and some winters, for the next five years. As in the earlier project, these were outstanding workers who ended up classifying most of our ceramics and many of our other materials, from obsidian to *manos* and *metates*.

More students worked on artifacts with the Yautepec project than with our earlier project at Capilco and Cuexcomate. Several students wrote PhD theses. Jan Olson, my student at the University at Albany, compared the household artifacts to study patterns of wealth inequality at Yautepec. Susan Norris wrote her PhD dissertation at Harvard on the obsidian workshops, and Ruth Fauman-Fichman completed a dissertation at the University of Pittsburgh on the cotton spinning tools. My students Lisa Montiel and Tim Hare wrote dissertations on an archaeological survey of the Yautepec Valley that we carried out shortly after the excavations. Several undergraduates at Albany wrote senior honors theses on artifacts from Yautepec, including studies of figurines, small ceramic objects, and imported Aztec pottery.

Flutes and whistles

The musical instruments we excavated at Yautepec were especially interesting to ancient music specialist Adje Both. Long after completion of the project, Adje came to Mexico as part of my team at Calixtlahuaca, my most recent fieldwork project. We spent several days together in the dusty labs in Cuernavaca and Yautepec so that he could study all of the musical instruments from Yautepec, Capilco, and Cuexcomate. His methods began with basic observations, measurements, and drawings. But then he would play any of the instruments that were intact. In a special form of experimental archaeology he recorded the sounds they could make, and analyzed the resulting sound diagrams for their musical and acoustic properties. When he had first applied this method to a big collection of whole flutes from offerings at the Templo Mayor of Tenochtitlan (López Luján 2005), Adje was able to disprove the common idea that the Aztec musical scale was pentatonic—that is, the notion that Aztec music only used five notes, corresponding to the black keys on a piano. In fact, Aztec musicians had a much fuller musical scale to work with, and their music was more sophisticated than people had thought previously (Both 2002, 2007).

Although we had excavated fragments of ceramic flutes, no complete examples had survived. A few of our whistles were complete, however. Of course, we had cleaned the dirt out of them in the field and had fun making them sound again after five centuries. A small whistle can only make a few sounds, but they can be quite loud. It is thrilling to be able to produce the same sounds that the original Aztec owners had produced 500 years ago. Adje recorded himself playing the whistles, and we now have the sound files as part of our project archives.

There is a rare and special kind of Aztec instrument known as a skull whistle, which prior to my excavations had only been reported from offerings at the main imperial temple of Tenochtitlan. This object is shaped like a human skull, and its wind passages are specially arranged to produce a kind of whooshing sound like a heavy wind in the trees. Although the technicalities are beyond me, Adje explained that the way the sound is produced in these skull whistles is unique in the world history of musical instruments. He had seen our photos of a skull whistle from Yautepec, and it was the first thing he looked for when we entered the lab together. After examining the object he made a video call to a colleague in Germany. I couldn't understand the conversation (in German), but it was clear that they were both talking excitedly about our skull whistle.

While my lab crew and I had classified and described our musical instruments in a competent fashion, Adje Both was able to glean much more information because of his training, his experience, and his use of specialized techniques like the analysis of sound diagrams. His work—done several years after we had finished up and officially closed the lab—shows the value of saving archaeological collections for future reference. If we had simply tossed out the artifacts upon completion of the project—a common occurrence in Mexico, given the current crisis in archaeological storage space—our whistles, flutes, rattles and bells would not have given up all of their secrets.

Obsidian workshops

It took archaeologists decades of trial and error to figure out how the Aztecs and other Mesoamerican peoples produced blades of obsidian. The technological knowledge had died out shortly after the Spanish Conquest. What archaeologists finally learned was that blade-making is a very difficult process, but the payoff was great: a freshly made obsidian blade has the sharpest edge known to science. Studies using an electron microscope show that a surgeon's scalpel is dull and rough compared to an obsidian blade. The process starts with a chunk of good quality obsidian, the size of a football or larger. The toolmaker uses a stone hammer to remove flakes and produce a "cylindrical core."

Once the cylindrical core is ready, the difficult part of the production process begins: removing the blades. Blades are long and thin, with sharp, parallel sides. The toolmaker has to apply great pressure to a specific point on the top of the core, very close to the edge. When enough pressure is applied, a blade pops off with a ping, and the toolmaker continues around the circumference of the core to remove the next blade. The hard part—the step that took decades to figure out—is applying enough pressure to exactly the right place. Arm strength is not enough: the rest of the body is required to produce enough force. In one method, the toolmaker sits on the ground with his legs extended. He holds the core between his feet, and positions a long pointed punch with his hands. The back of the punch, attached to a butt or cross-piece, is placed against the chest. Then the toolmaker leans forward to apply the force.

Eventually the removal of the blades takes less force, and the toolmaker can use his or her arm strength and work in a more comfortable position (Figure 6.4). After some 200 blades have been removed from a core, the toolmaker either tosses the used-up core into the trash (to perhaps turn up centuries later in an archaeologist's screen), or else he gives it to a colleague to make into an ear-spool, a lip-plug, or some other item of jewelry (Andrews 2008). The fact that we found obsidian cores at Yautepec but not at Capilco or Cuexcomate showed that the city was a place for tool production, unlike the rural sites.

After participating in the excavations in 1993, Albany undergraduate Sue Norris went on to graduate study at Harvard University. After getting the proper training, Sue spent several years working on the Yautepec obsidian. She found that during the Settlement Period, none of the middens had any evidence for blade production. In the Growth Period, however, four of the ten houses yielded debris from blade production, as did four of the twelve middens from the Imperial Period. The single house with a midden from the Spanish Period was also the home of obsidian workers. And during the Growth and Imperial Periods one house was the setting for the manufacture of obsidian jewelry.

Sue's study uncovered two valuable insights about the economy of ancient Yautepec. Craftsmen produced obsidian tools at home, where the waste materials ended up with the household trash in a midden. And some but not all of the households had resident toolmakers. The manufacture of prismatic blades was a specialized and demanding skill, something that not just anyone could pick up without extensive training.

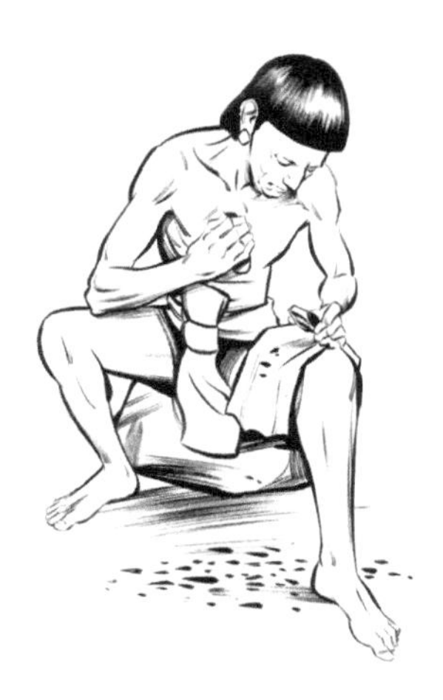

FIGURE 6.4 An obsidian knapper at work. Drawing by Kagan McLeod.

I recall one morning during the excavations when our group of local women were washing the obsidian artifacts in the lab. They quickly learned to be careful with the sharp edges. These women would gossip while they washed artifacts. They had somehow got the idea that Cindy was my Mexican mistress, while I had a wife and family back in the U.S. In their eyes, this made me quite the macho. But in Mexico an even higher level of machismo comes when a man supports two entire families: his wife and official children, plus a mistress and her children. One morning, a school holiday, April and Heather came out to Yautepec with us, and this caused a stir among the sherd washers.

"Isn't he macho? Two families—wow that's really something!"

One of the students overheard this and set them straight. "Dr. Smith has just one wife and just two children, and they are all right here in the lab." My machismo level plummeted, and the women seemed a bit sheepish the rest of the day.

Scientific studies of trade

The Aztec way of life depended on trade and markets. Many farmers cultivated cotton, which meant they had to trade with others for maize, beans, and other foods. Obsidian workers and other urban specialists exchanged their products for food in the market. The study of ancient trade and markets has been revolutionized in the past decade by the application of advanced techniques of chemical analysis. We can now pinpoint the places of origin of many goods, and obsidian is the best example.

There are only twenty or so places in central Mexico where obsidian occurs naturally. The obsidian from each geological source can be identified using advanced techniques, such as X-ray fluorescence or induced neutron activation analysis.

For Capilco and Cuexcomate, I had not carried out any chemical testing of obsidian. More than nine-tenths of the artifacts had a green tint. This meant that I could trace the samples to a known mountain-top obsidian source near Pachuca, north of Mexico City, the only source of green obsidian. At Yautepec green obsidian was also dominant—between 90 and 94 percent—but now it seemed worthwhile to carry out some chemical tests focusing on the gray obsidian. The reason for my change in strategy was a breakthrough in the archaeological analysis of ancient market systems.

Although written sources on Aztec cities mention markets and merchants, the lack of documents from rural and provincial areas meant that I could not be sure whether markets were operating at my sites or not. One result of the growth of household archaeology was that in the 1990s archaeologists began to devise strategies to identify market exchange using household data (Garraty and Stark 2010; Hirth 1998). Many of these methods are based on comparison of the quantities of different artifacts among households. With these new methods, I could use the results of chemical analysis of obsidian to test whether markets operated in Yautepec.

I had students select six pieces of gray obsidian at random from each house occupied during each period. I exported the samples to the States, and Adrian Burke, then a graduate student at the University at Albany, analyzed their trace elements using a method called X-ray fluorescence. He identified the likely geological sources, and then we confirmed his results by having some of the pieces analyzed again at the Missouri University Research Reactor, the top obsidian lab in the U.S.

Adrian's analysis had three results that supported the hypothesis that people bought their obsidian in the markets. First, many different sources of gray obsidian were represented among the Yautepec households. This material came from a variety of places throughout central Mexico, all more than 100 miles away. If obsidian was instead being supplied by elites or the government, we would expect fewer source areas. Second, each household had gray obsidian from three to five different sources, and the specific combinations were different at each house. Again, if households were getting their obsidian from a central authority, they would probably all have similar collections of material. Instead, families must have attended the market to buy their obsidian, where they purchased whatever material happened to be on sale that day. Since families would make their purchases at different times throughout the year, they each ended up with a slightly different collection of types of gray obsidian. The third pattern is that obsidian from a variety of sources turned up in both commoner and elite middens.

Taken together, these results of the chemical analysis of gray obsidian give some of the strongest evidence for my claim that markets operated at Yautepec. One very interesting result was identifying the presence of tools of obsidian from sources within the Tarascan Empire, mortal enemy of the Aztecs. These objects entered the Mexica Empire through the same black-market channels that brought Tarascan bronze to sites in Morelos. Smuggling and contraband are nothing new. They have been around since the first kings decided to control trade in their kingdom.

The Yautepec excavations turned up thirty-one bronze tools very similar to the needles and other objects recovered at Capilco and Cuexcomate. Dorothy Hosler, the bronze expert from M.I.T., analyzed this collection, too, carrying out advanced chemical analysis of the objects. Although it is not possible to pinpoint the place of origin of bronze in the manner of obsidian, her lead isotope analysis revealed that the Yautepec artifacts were indeed made in the Tarascan area of western Mexico (Hosler 1994; Hosler and Macfarlane 1996).

One of Dorothy's visits to Cuernavaca came while she was returning from a trip to southern Mexico to study native methods of extracting rubber. She had found some peasants in an out-of-the-way jungle village who still extracted and processed rubber as the Aztecs and Mayas had done centuries ago. This helped scholars understand how the ancient Mesoamericans had played their ritual ballgame (Tarkanian and Hosler 2011). Dorothy watched these modern rubber-workers make some large rubber balls and carried them back to M.I.T. in gallon paint cans. While at our house in Cuernavaca, she opened one of the cans to show Cindy and me what the rubber was like. The ball was the size of a softball, but soft, squishy, and greasy. I threw it down on the driveway, and to my surprise it bounced high, like a superball. Dorothy didn't mind this, but when our landlord's dogs—a couple of big, exuberant German Shepherds—started to chase the ball, I had to put it back in the can. The dogs evidently agreed with me: experimental archaeology can be fun.

Life in the big city

How did urban life at Yautepec differ from rural life at Cuexcomate and Capilco? First, the bad news about Aztec urban life: higher taxes. Most taxes were paid in cotton textiles and the amounts were fixed and recorded on bark-paper tax lists. These were similar for urban and rural residents. But people also had to pay labor taxes, and these were less regular. Labor gangs were called up when needed, for all kinds of tasks, from digging an irrigation canal to cleaning the plaza after a ceremony. Urban residents were far more likely to be called up for these labor taxes than rural people, just because they lived in town and were easier to round up.

The positive features of Aztec urban life came from the higher levels of economic activity. People had more opportunities to work as craft specialists in the city, and the presence of urban workshops meant that obsidian blades and other craft items were more readily available to consumers (and probably cheaper, too). Urban marketplaces were larger and busier than those held in the countryside. Markets were held more frequently and traveling merchants more likely to sell at urban markets. Also, it was easier for urban residents to set up a market stall and sell their family's craft products, prepared tacos, or other items. In all, urban markets offered more goods for sale, and more opportunities for economic activity. The presence of cacao vessels at Yautepec, but not the rural sites, shows that people took advantage of these opportunities. Overall, urban life held both attractions and disadvantages to commoners.

The three main time periods defined for the rural sites—Settlement (AD 1100–1300), Growth (1300–1430), and Imperial (1430–1521)—appeared to fit Yautepec as well. But since the ceramic types at Yautepec were different, I had to go through another round of chronology building to make sure. This time my student Timothy Hare helped out with the computer seriation, stratigraphy, and radiocarbon dates. We defined four local periods, of which the first three had almost identical calendar dates to the equivalent periods at Capilco and Cuexcomate. We also added Santiago as the period after the arrival of Cortés in Hare and Smith (1996).

The city of Yautepec followed the same developmental path as Capilco and Cuexcomate. The city was founded in the Settlement Period, and several of the excavated houses were built and occupied at this time. In the Growth Period, the city expanded greatly. The earlier houses continued to be used, and many more were built. Expansion continued into the Imperial Period.

As at the rural sites, urban houses did not change at all after Mexica conquest, and the middens showed little transformation in domestic activities or conditions. The biggest change was a drop in the amount of obsidian people in Yautepec had in their homes. The types of obsidian tools did not change, nor did the number of obsidian workshops. But overall, people kept less obsidian around the house during the Imperial Period than in either of the two earlier periods. While I cannot explain the drop, it seems clear that Yautepec, like the rural sites, was resilient in the face of Aztec conquest. And given the overall prominence of imported and valuable goods—in all three pre-Spanish periods—it is not hard to conclude that Yautepec was a successful and sustainable settlement, again, like the rural sites. But this situation would change radically with the arrival of Cortés in 1519.

Cortés and the Spanish conquest

The story of the conquest of Mexico is well known; I summarize it in my textbook (Smith 2012: chapter 13). Several hundred Spanish soldiers of fortune, under the leadership of Hernan Cortés, landed in Mexico in 1519. Within two years, the Mexica Empire was in shambles and Spaniards ruled the land. The peoples of Morelos played a small role in the Spanish conquest. After an initial setback, Cortés launched his final destructive attack on Tenochtitlan by marching first through Morelos to make sure the local kings would not come to the aid of the Mexica Empire. The rulers of the leading Morelos city-states—including Yautepec—surrendered to him without fuss. By the time his army of Spaniards and native allies reached the lakeshore and began their siege of the capital, smallpox had arrived in Mexico. Things worsened when Cortés shut off the aqueduct that brought fresh water into the capital. On August 13, 1521, after months of battle, the last emperor—Cuauhtemoc—was captured and Cortés claimed victory.

The smallpox that devastated Tenochtitlan in its final months was only the first in a series of deadly epidemics that spread through Mexico (and the entire New World) in the century after 1521. Regardless of the specific actions of Cortés and Motecuhzoma, the Mexica Empire was doomed, and in the aftermath of Spanish conquest, the households and communities that are the focus of my story did not stand a chance.

The native population of Morelos—and all of Mexico—dropped precipitously after 1521. Those natives who survived were grouped into estates known as *encomiendas*, under the control of a Spaniard. Some were sent to work in mines and others worked on sugar cane plantations. Aztec settlements had been scattered across the landscape, and Spanish officials began moving rural people into new towns. They did this to convert people to Christianity and to control them more effectively. The remaining residents of Capilco and Cuexcomate were moved into the new village of Tetlama, whose small sixteenth-century church still stands. Within a few decades of the Spanish conquest, Capilco and Cuexcomate lay in ruins. The workers I hired from Tetlama were excavating the houses of their distant ancestors at Capilco and Cuexcomate.

As an important city in a fertile valley, Yautepec was quickly taken over by Spaniards. Some moved into the city center, and the friars built the churches where I excavated over four centuries later. The midden next to House 3 shows that, for some commoners at least, many aspects of pre-Spanish life continued. People also had access to new products and animals brought from Spain. The midden contained glazed pottery, iron nails, and cow and horse bones, in addition to the basic Imperial Period artifacts. The irrigated maize and cotton fields in the Yautepec Valley were quickly replanted with sugar cane, and most of the commoners in

Yautepec and its former city-state territory were put to work producing sugar for the sixteenth-century world market. Life was not good for these plantation workers. They were little better than slaves, forced to labor and lacking the resources to decide their own destiny. Those who did not die from the epidemics that swept through central Mexico between 1521 and 1700 had to work even harder to keep up. While the Aztec market system had been a positive force in the lives of the farmers of Morelos, the combination of cruel landlords and an unforgiving world market for sugar in the Spanish Period worked against the well-being of the people of Yautepec.

7

RESILIENT COMMUNITIES

For a long time, the concept of community was missing from my thinking about the Morelos settlements. When I finished up lab work at Yautepec I was unwilling or unable to evaluate the Morelos sites as communities. My first task was to write up the results of both fieldwork projects, a process that took five years. I had to describe these excavations—in minute detail—in Spanish-language reports to the Mexican government. By the time this was done I was burned out. I didn't care whether the people who had lived in those excavated houses were rich, poor, happy, sad, resilient, or downtrodden. I had excavated their houses, I had described it all in great detail, and I was ready for something new.

When the opportunity came in 2005 to take a job at Arizona State University in Tempe, I jumped at it. It was an easy choice: ASU has one of the best archaeology programs in the U.S., and Cindy had always wanted to live in the southwest. Our girls were grown up with lives of their own. If they want to drink from the garden hose now, that's their problem, not ours. My move to ASU opened up two new research projects, and these in turn led me back to the past, back to the Morelos fieldwork described in this book. And taking a fresh look at these sites allowed me to understand them deeply for the first time.

My first new project was an excavation of Calixtlahuaca, an Aztec provincial city in the Toluca Valley west of the Valley of Mexico (Smith et al. 2013, 2009). Although occupied at the same time as the Morelos settlements, Calixtlahuaca differed from those sites in many ways. It was a larger and far more powerful city than Yautepec, but its residents had a lower quality of life than the people of Morelos. They had fewer imported goods and fewer shared styles than the commoners of Capilco, Cuexcomate, and Yautepec. The conquest of Calixtlahuaca by the Mexica Empire was far more devastating than in Morelos. These and other comparisons would help me figure out how and why Capilco, Cuexcomate, and Yautepec were such remarkable and successful communities.

My second new project was a collaborative study of urban neighborhoods, from the earliest cities to the present. ASU promotes research that cuts across the lines of traditional fields of scholarship, and I joined a group of six professors and a number of students to study neighborhood organization. Our faculty group consisted of three archaeologists, a political scientist, a geographer, and a sociologist.

By comparing urban neighborhoods from deep history to the present, using the skills of archaeology, history, geography, sociology, and political science, we learned two things. First, all cities have neighborhood organization. This is one of the few universals of urban life. We also discovered that neighborhoods can form through two radically different paths. In the top-down route, civil authorities create neighborhoods for their own purposes. In earlier times this meant that city officials would set up and regulate neighborhoods. Today the top-down approach is associated with real-estate developers whose planned residential communities feature built-in neighborhoods even before anyone moves in. In the bottom-up path, by contrast, urban residents create their own neighborhoods through their daily activities, without much help or interference from the government. Not surprisingly, life seems more vibrant and people more satisfied in neighborhoods that form the bottom-up way.[1]

I began to study urban neighborhoods at Aztec cities. Rather unexpectedly, the same form of Aztec community organization—the *calpolli*—was prominent in both rural and rural contexts. In cities, a *calpolli* was a neighborhood, and in the countryside, it was a village or a town. Some of the best information on the nature of the Aztec *calpolli* comes from historical documents from six communities in Morelos. Back when we excavated at Capilco and Cuexcomate it had occurred to me that these sites may correspond to *calpollis*, but I had not realized that this was the key to their success and resilience. By taking another look at *calpollis* in our comparative neighborhoods project, the pieces fell into place. The Aztec *calpollis* were in effect neighborhoods generated by bottom-up processes. They shaped the actions of their members in ways that led to success and resilience.

To explain why this matters—and why I can claim these Aztec communities were successful and resilient—I begin with the idea of community.

What is a community?

Capilco, Cuexcomate, and Yautepec are archaeological sites today, but six centuries ago they were communities. They were places where people spent their lives working, relaxing and interacting with their neighbors. People got together to gossip about their neighbors, to talk about crops, the weather, and the goods for sale at the market that week, or the pending arrival of the greedy imperial tax collector. But these communities were not just places where people lived. They were settings where people worked together toward common goals. The *calpolli* mattered because it helped people reach these goals.

Research by anthropologists, sociologists, and other social scientists has led to a new understanding of the nature of communities—whether they are Aztec villages or modern gated neighborhoods. Communities—in the past and present—form mainly through social interaction. Sharing common values or having a distinct community identity might be important in some places, but interacting socially is important in all of them. Economists Samuel Bowles and Herbert Gintis, recognized for their contributions to the study of communities and social cooperation, offer this definition:

> By community we mean a group of people who interact directly, frequently and in multi-faceted ways. People who work together are usually communities in this sense, as are some neighborhoods, groups of friends, professional and business networks, gangs, and sports leagues. The list suggests that connection, not affection, is the defining characteristic of a community. Whether one is born into a community or one entered by choice, there are normally significant costs to moving from one to another.
>
> *(Bowles and Gintis 2002: F420). See also Flint (2009)*

Today, some communities are not tied to a particular geographic location; online communities can link people in widely scattered places. But in traditional societies both past and present, communities consist of people living in a single place and interacting face-to-face. Even in today's online world, face-to-face interactions remain important (Ostrom 1990; Sampson 2012). In the worlds of economist Edward Glaeser, "Our social species' greatest talent is the ability to learn from each other, and we learn more deeply and thoroughly when we're face-to-face" (Glaeser 2011: 250).

When I returned to the Morelos communities after moving to ASU, I wanted to evaluate their success using archaeological evidence, so I devised four measures: prosperity, persistence, stability, and resilience to conquest. Understanding these four measures helps answer the question of why these communities and their households succeeded so well.

Prosperous communities

Although archaeological remains are silent about the friendship, gossip, and visiting that lie at the heart of social interaction and cohesion in communities, they *can* tell us about people working together to accomplish common goals. Collective construction projects improved the lives of the residents of Capilco, Cuexcomate, and Yautepec by building cohesion and trust. Today, the ruins of civic and agricultural projects offer silent testimony of the prosperity of these communities. In the modern world, most construction work is done by businesses using wage labor. People might build their own houses—a common practice in the developing world—but collective work on large projects is rare.

Barn-raising parties were once common, and they still flourish among the Amish. As sustainability writer Bill McKibben observes, "working together is not some freak Amish trait—it's what all people did before they had machinery powerful enough to enable them to work alone" (McKibben 2007: 116). But I am talking about a different kind of collective labor. For the Amish, working on a neighbor's barn was a form of exchange among households. People helped one another out, but they were not building something larger that served the community as a whole. Perhaps the closest modern analogs to ancient joint construction projects are cases where community members turn out to build a playground or clean up a park. Whether talking about neighbors renovating a park today or *calpolli* members constructing a temple or canal five centuries ago, the ability of people to solve collective problems is one of the measures of successful communities, according to Bowles and Gintis.

I found evidence for at least two sets of collective construction projects at each of the excavated sites. Capilco sits at the base of a hill, and its residents dug a long diversion ditch upslope from the village to catch rainwater that would have flooded the village. Since this feature benefits the entire village, its construction was probably organized above the level of a single household.

The check-dam terraces themselves were a collective construction project, but only in a limited fashion. The irregular patterns and small scale of the walls show that the planning and construction of the terraces at Capilco and Cuexcomate were not organized by a central authority. Nevertheless, individual households had to find some way to coordinate their activities, if only to keep disputes in check and make sure that a rainstorm didn't wash away an entire zone of terraces. Maybe neighboring farmers simply agreed to collaborate, or perhaps the job was coordinated by the *calpolli*. But in either case, the residents of Capilco worked together to improve their community.

At Cuexcomate, terracing also indicates social interaction, but at this town site the civic architecture shows an even higher level of collaboration and coordination among households. At the time of the Mexica conquest, "downtown" Cuexcomate consisted of a noble compound (Group 6), a small temple, a special residence, and a public plaza (Figure 7.1, top). The construction of each civic building was a major collective project. The noble who lived in Group 6 organized the planning and construction of this civic center. After the Mexica conquest Group 6 was abandoned and a new, smaller noble compound was built (Group 7), and the temple was enlarged (Figure 7.1, bottom). These new construction activities show that the collective work of the residents of Cuexcomate continued into the Imperial Period, even after a change in the noble household living on the plaza. Terracing and temple construction were very different kinds of collective projects, one organized by neighbors, from the bottom up, the other a top-down and enforced process. But they both signal the prosperity of the community of Cuexcomate. People worked together toward a common end, and the places they created improved the town and benefitted everyone.

Construction of the royal palace and nearby civic architecture at Yautepec must have been directed by the king or his agents, as these projects were much larger

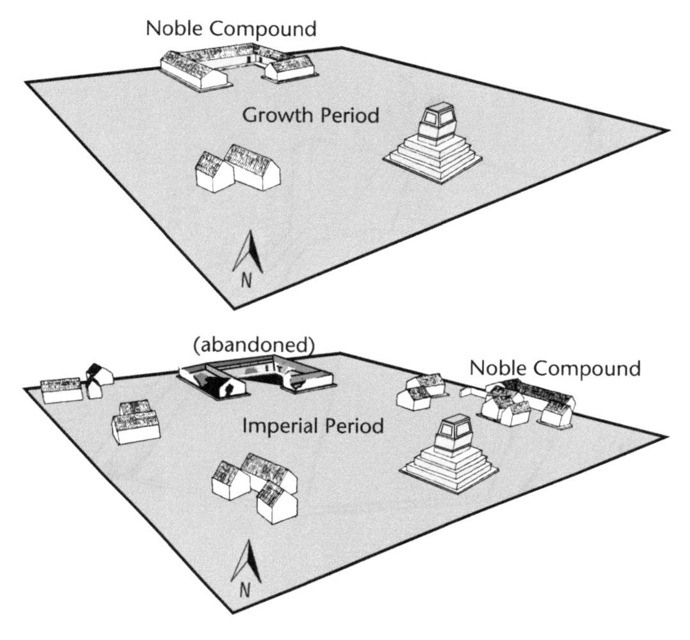

FIGURE 7.1 Civic architecture around the plaza at Cuexcomate. Top: Growth Period 1300–1430); bottom: Imperial Period (1430–1520). Drawing by Shelby Manney.

than anything at the country town of Cuexcomate. Compared to the 500 square meter size of the Cuexcomate palace, the Yautepec royal palace covered more than 6,000 square meters. Yautepec was divided into neighborhoods. Based on other Aztec cities, it is very likely that each neighborhood had a small civic center with a temple, a school and a small plaza. Unfortunately this small-scale civic architecture has not survived at Yautepec (Figure 7.2).

A third kind of collective construction project at Yautepec was the infrastructure of the irrigation system. There is no direct evidence to determine whether the *calpolli* supervised the construction of dams and canals or whether agents of the king took control, but the end result was the same—a collective project whose construction and use signaled the prosperity of the neighborhoods and city of Yautepec.

Five hundred years ago, these Aztec communities were doing things that experts recommend for the improvement of communities and neighborhoods today. In a chapter called "All for One, One for All," Bill McKibben promotes shared activities and work toward common goals as ways to improve people's lives. Similarly, community development experts John McKnight and Peter Block encourage families and neighborhoods to take charge of local affairs by working together in many realms of life (McKibben 2007; McKnight and Block 2010). These ancient Aztec farmers didn't need experts to tell them how to improve their communities. They figured this out on their own.

FIGURE 7.2 Building a neighborhood temple at Yautepec. Drawing by Kagan McLeod.

Long-lasting communities

Successful and prosperous communities—ancient and modern—persist for long periods of time. Community survival is much easier in the modern world because government policies, private property, and the insurance industry ensure that even destroyed communities will rebuild and survive. Think of New Orleans after Hurricane Katrina, or towns in the Midwestern U.S. devastated by tornados or floods. In ancient times, if a community was destroyed or abandoned, no one gave it a second thought. Historians who have studied early American utopian communities—towns like the Shaker settlements founded by charismatic leaders for religious or moral purposes—use their longevity or duration as one measure of their success. Some of these communities were successful and lasted for many decades, while some fell apart after a few years. The fact that the Morelos communities I excavated persisted in time for several centuries is an indication of their success.

Capilco lasted 450 years, Cuexcomate 250 years, and Yautepec is still thriving after more than 900 years. Compared to some ancient communities these are relatively short occupations. Several towns in the Yautepec Valley, founded before the time of Christ, were occupied continuously for nearly 2,000 years! But the crucial fact is that once these Aztec communities were founded they continued to thrive at least until the Spanish conquest. For the period before Cortés arrived, Capilco, Cuexcomate, and Yautepec each achieved its maximum possible age, without any episodes of abandonment.

But these communities did not just survive for centuries; they thrived and they grew. Except for a major population decline at Yautepec *after* the Spanish conquest, each settlement showed steady growth over its history. Capilco was founded by around thirty people, and though it grew continuously, it remained a village for its entire history. The founding of Cuexcomate as a town two centuries later was a bigger deal. About 200 commoners and a family of nobles arrived together, and by the Spanish conquest, Cuexcomate had grown to 800 residents. Yautepec was a city from the start, growing to a maximum Imperial Period size of around 15,000 people, and it remains a city today. Although ancient growth is usually considered a sign of success, in the Buenavista hills population may have grown too rapidly, leading to a slight decline in the quality of life. Unlike the rich Yautepec Valley, this was a difficult environment to farm, and by the Imperial Period the negative consequences of growth (a slight decline in the quality of life) had started to set in.

Stable communities

The Morelos communities did not just persist for centuries; their membership and composition were remarkably stable during that time. The irrigation canals in Yautepec and the terracing that surrounded Cuexcomate and Capilco offer concrete evidence for social stability. Anthropologist Robert Netting studied peasant farmers around the world and found that they only invest in such improvements to the landscape when communities are stable and individual households have secure access to their fields year after year (Netting 1993). Otherwise, such farmers, called smallholders for the size of their fields, do not consider it worth the effort to improve the landscapes of their farms with walls and canals. The residents of the Morelos communities are good examples of Netting's smallholders category.

Residential stability is an important ingredient of successful communities today. Not surprisingly, sociologists have discovered that urban neighborhoods where people move frequently have higher rates of crime and poverty than more stable neighborhoods (Hanson 2005; Sampson 2012):

> Residential stability enhances social integration and the likelihood that residents know each other, whereas residential mobility raises the likelihood that neighbors feel estranged from each other and weakens the capacity for collective action with respect to local issues. A greater concentration of long-term residents may foster a social climate in which people establish familiar, enduring bonds.
>
> *(Schieman 2005: 1034)*

As an archaeologist I cannot trace the movement of individuals or households within or between settlements, but I do have a reliable—if cruder—measure of stability: continuity in the occupation of individual houses. Did people continue to occupy houses from one period into the next? Or were houses abandoned as people left to try their luck elsewhere? When I graphed the house occupations through time for Capilco and Cuexcomate, I was surprised at the remarkable levels of continuity.

With the exception of the noble compound, no house was abandoned before the Spanish conquest. Once a house was built and occupied, people continued living in it until the end of the Imperial Period. When I moved my excavations to Yautepec, I figured that urban households and communities would be less stable than their rural counterparts. My assumption was incorrect: the house occupations for Yautepec were also stable, with a continuity rate of 100 percent (Figure 7.3). I did not realize how remarkable this stability was until I started excavating at Calixtlahuaca, where many houses were abandoned at the end of each period.

This continuity suggests that all three places enjoyed a high level of social stability. Planners and architects in the New Urbanism movement would be pleased with these communities as they illustrate some of its basic principles: "long life and permanence, rather than transience" and creation of "a culture of permanence" in housing. The new urbanists are trying to improve modern communities by making them more sociable and sustainable. These principles of permanence are laid out in the "Canons of Sustainable Architecture and Urbanism," a publication by the Congress for the New Urbanism. The new urbanists, like Bill McKibben, recognize that the sense of community has declined in many cities with rising individualism and automobile dependence (Congress for the New Urbanism 2008: 2–3). Perhaps these Aztec communities offer lessons in successful community design.

The single exception to this stable occupation is the nobles' residence, Group 6, at Cuexcomate. This compound was abandoned and a smaller and far less luxurious replacement was built on the north side of the plaza. The only logical explanation for this move is an external conquest: the Buenavista hills were conquered twice in the early fifteenth century. First, the expanding Cuauhnahuac (Cuernavaca) city-state

FIGURE 7.3 An excavated house (structure 4) at Yautepec. Photograph by Michael E. Smith.

conquered the Buenavista hills sometime around 1400. Then in the 1430s the Mexica Empire conquered Cuauhnahuac and all of Morelos. Although my chronology is not refined enough to identify which of these two conquests was responsible for the demise of Group 6, the smaller Group 7 replaced it as the central compound in the Imperial Period. It is probably no coincidence that residential stability was greater among the commoners of Cuexcomate than among their elite landlords.

Resilient communities

Perhaps the best indication that the Morelos communities were prosperous and successful is that they weathered the Mexica conquest. The technical term for this is *resilience*, a concept developed by engineers and ecologists to describe physical systems and ecosystems that can withstand external shocks and retain their basic operation. For human communities resilience is the ability of a community to cope with serious external disturbances and maintain its basic features and operations (Adger 2000: 347; Tainter and Taylor 2014). The major external shocks that affected these sites were conquests. How did the communities of Capilco, Cuexcomate, and Yautepec respond to the shocks of the Mexica and Spanish conquests of Morelos?

The answers are clear from archaeology and history: these sites easily survived Mexica conquest, but the Spanish conquest destroyed them. Mexica conquest brought a few changes in the quantities of imported ceramics at all sites, but these were minor shifts. Textile production went up at Cuexcomate but declined at the other two sites. The amount of obsidian declined at Yautepec, but went up at the rural sites. The standard of living, as measured from artifacts, declined slightly at all three sites.

The Spanish conquest, on the other hand, was highly destructive. Capilco and Cuexcomate were abandoned. Those residents who did not die of smallpox were taken to the new town of Tetlama. Farmers stopped using the terraces, and men were sent to other parts of Mexico to work for the Spaniards in mines and haciendas. Yautepec continued to be occupied in the Spanish Period, but with major social disruptions. Our lone Spanish Period house was built in the Imperial Period and continued to be occupied across the Spanish conquest. New Spanish items showed up in the midden, including iron tools, glazed ceramics, and bones from cows and horses. But the majority of the domestic items were the standard artifacts of the Imperial Period. It appears that this house was abandoned after a few decades of Spanish rule, and it provides only a limited view of Spanish Period life in Yautepec. Historical documents from throughout central Mexico tell us that the lives of both commoners and nobles deteriorated under Spanish rule, and the most logical conclusion is that the Spanish conquest had a significant negative impact on Yautepec.

Did all central Mexican communities have similar responses to conquest—resilient to the Mexica but not the Spanish conquest? It turns out that the only other Aztec sites with enough house excavations to make this comparison—Calixtlahuaca and Xaltocan—were *not* resilient to Mexica conquest. My recent excavations at Calixtlahuaca found that many houses were abandoned and others established anew in the Imperial Period. There was a major change in diet, perhaps due to an influx of immigrants from the Valley of Mexico with different food preferences who took over the city. The case of Xaltocan, an island city in the northern Valley of Mexico, is more complicated. Sometime close to the rise of the Mexica Empire, the intensive and highly productive agricultural raised fields that fed Xaltocan were abandoned, probably a casualty of Mexica meddling or suppression. Genetic evidence from burials shows that new people moved in.

Their stories are different, but Calixtlahuaca and Xaltocan both suffered greatly after their incorporation into the Mexica Empire (Mata-Míguez et al. 2012; Morehart 2012; Smith et al. 2009, 2013). In contrast, the Morelos communities thrived for centuries, their populations grew steadily, and the Mexica conquest had little effect. Xaltocan and Calixtlahuaca show that not all places survived Mexica conquest unscathed. The difference between these two sites and those in Morelos had less to do with imperial policy than with the local conditions that made the latter communities more resilient to external shocks. Among those local conditions, two institutions stand out—the *calpolli* and the city-state.

The *calpolli:* key to community success

In the 1540s, two decades after the fall of Tenochtitlan, a Spanish administrator ordered a series of census reports from six towns in Morelos. He assembled a team of Nahuatl-speaking scribes to go from house to house asking questions about residents, land holdings and taxes. They recorded the information, along with the names and kin relationships of the residents, in Nahuatl written in the European script. These documents furnish a detailed picture of the nature of households and *calpollis* in Morelos soon after the Spanish conquest (Carrasco 1976; McCaa 2003). Here is the entry for one house in the village of Quauhchichinollan (located a few miles southwest of Capilco and Cuexcomate):

> Ninth house. Here is the home of one named Huitznahuatl. His wife is named Necahual. He has two children. The first one is named Tlaco, now ten years old. The second is named Quauhtitlan, now five years old. Here is Huitznahuatl's brother-in-law named Ilhuitl, now twenty years old, not yet married. He is still a bachelor and just accompanies Huitznahuatl. Here is Huitznahuatl's nephew. He has two children. Huitznahuatl's niece is just a widow. Two years ago her husband died. She has one child, now five years old. The widow is named Tecapan. Here is Huitznahuatl's older sister, who just accompanies him. She is just an abandoned person; she was married someplace else. Her name is Tlaco. Here is his field: 20 matl long and 15 matl wide. Here is the tribute [rent]: every 80 days they deliver together one quarter-length of a Cuernavaca cloak and in addition, one quarter-length of a tribute cloak, and one quarter-length of a narrow cloak. That is all. No turkey hens, no turkey eggs. There are thirteen included here.
>
> *(Cline 1993: 137–139)*

Huitznahuatl's household was an extended family of thirteen living in a single house compound. This was the most common form of family in the six communities. Where it says that his brother-in-law and older sister "accompany" Huitznahuatl, it means they helped with the work of the farm.

While scholars knew about *calpollis* for centuries (and argued furiously about them), no one seemed to recognize just how important they were for the prosperity of Aztec households and communities until anthropologist Pedro Carrasco found these Nahuatl-language documents in a dusty archive in Mexico City in the 1960s. Pedro and his family had fled fascist Spain in the wake of the Spanish civil war. After some time in Mexico, he moved to the U.S. where he gained a Ph.D. and then a distinguished teaching career. Pedro knew from his experience in Spain about the struggles between local communities and the central state, and he dedicated his career to exploring this theme using documents on Aztec society. He immediately recognized the value of this house-by-house census of six communities. It turns out that many commoner households included non-kin boarders who helped with the farm work. Other households consisted of small nuclear families. Noblemen, on the other hand, typically lived with several wives and their children, sometimes a concubine or two, as well as servants and other domestic helpers.

Quauhchichinollan and the other communities in these documents resembled those I had excavated. One of them, in fact—a *calpolli* called Molotla—was a neighborhood of Yautepec. I never managed to figure out where it was located on the ground, but I like to imagine that some of the older people in the census may have grown up in a house I excavated in Yautepec. The only obvious social change introduced by the Spaniards was that some of the residents had been baptized as Christians. When I applied Pedro Carrasco's insights about the census material to my archaeological remains, the full explanation for the success of the Morelos households and communities fell into place.

The households in each census were listed by *calpolli*. A *calpolli* was a community of commoner households living near one another and subject to the same noble patron, who owned the land. The *calpolli* was run by a council of household heads. They allocated plots of land to members and made decisions about membership. New members had to be approved by the council, and if a farmer abandoned his plot for a year or two, he could be expelled from the *calpolli* (Lockhart 1992; Smith 1993).

The *calpolli* helped protect commoners, guaranteeing them access to land and providing some shelter from the demands of nobles and kings. But *calpollis* were not universal. Present in Morelos and the Basin of Mexico, they were largely absent from other regions, which left commoners in those areas more open to exploitation. Farmers who belonged to a *calpolli* had some say over their farms and their lives, whereas those without a *calpolli* were more like medieval European serfs—impoverished and subject to the whims of nobles. The flexibility and local control afforded by the *calpolli* are the final piece of my explanation for the high quality of life of Morelos households, and for the resilience and success of Morelos communities.

Although archaeology cannot prove *calpollis* existed at the sites I excavated, several lines of evidence support this idea. The census documents reveal *calpolli* organization in all types of settlements, from villages to cities, and one of those six communities was a neighborhood of Yautepec. Also, the numbers of houses at Capilco and Cuexcomate closely match the average number of households per *calpolli* in the documents. These documents reveal *calpollis* came in two sizes: small *calpollis* contained around twenty households, and several together composed a large *calpolli* with about 150 households. The village of Capilco, with its twenty houses, matches the small type, and the town of Cuexcomate—with 150 houses, a resident noble household, and a temple—corresponds to the larger type. The city of Yautepec must have contained ten to fifteen large *calpolli*. The *calpolli* is one of the main reasons for the success of Aztec communities in Morelos.

Responsive local government: the city-state

Aztec *calpollis* were grouped into city-states. The local city-state was a far more important level of government for the Aztec people than was the Mexica Empire. Men went to war for their city-state king, not for the imperial emperor. People paid most of their taxes to their local king. City-state governments kept track of births, deaths, marriages, and land holdings. People were protected by the patron god of their city-state, not by the imperial high gods. Most commoners married spouses from their city-state. Peasants went to their city-state capital, not Tenochtitlan, to take care of their business, both official and social.

Social historian Charles Tilly used to say that governments do two things: they exploit people and they provide services (Tilly 1985). From the earliest states in ancient Mesopotamia 5,000 years ago to the contemporary world, the relationships between people and their government can be judged by these two measures. Tally up the levels of exploitation and services in Aztec city-states and it looks like most people received a fair deal. Compared to the Mexica Empire protection racket, city-states played a far more positive role in commoner life. Tax levels were not particularly high, and people gained much from their city-state: military protection, courts and judges, promotion of commerce, and construction of infrastructure. Kings knew that if they pushed too hard, people could move away. Or they could start shopping at competing markets in nearby city-states, or perhaps shirk on their taxes and other obligations.

If we imagine governments arranged along a scale from despotic to democratic, the Aztec city-states would lie somewhere in the middle, leaning slightly toward the democratic side. These were not democracies in any sense of the term, but the *calpolli* gave people some say in local affairs, and some level of control over their lives. The level of exploitation in the city-states was not too high. Aztec commoners had fewer freedoms and less control of their government than did the Classical Greeks, but they were far ahead of their distant cousins in ancient Egypt, Babylonia, Inca Peru, and many other despotic states of antiquity (Blanton and Fargher 2008; Trigger 2003). The relative freedom of most Aztec commoners and the responsiveness of city-state government were key ingredients in the success of the Morelos communities.

Far from poor, downtrodden peasants, the people whose houses I excavated in Morelos were prosperous members of dynamic and successful communities. While elites and the Mexica Empire exploited these people, several things allowed them to thrive. The *calpolli* gave local communities flexibility and enough local control to organize farming and other activities to their advantage. The city-state provided some services and allowed *calpollis* to flourish. People had resources—soil and water—needed to grow food and cultivate cotton. And the market system linked people with the outside world and transformed local cotton into imports and wealth.

Note

1 For more information, see our project website: (http://cities.wikispaces.asu.edu/).

8

LESSONS FROM THE DIRT

This book began with three mysteries. I was a young archaeologist directing my first excavation project, and many of my ideas about what I might find when we started digging were incorrect. This led to my initial puzzlement about bronze needles, agricultural terraces, and musical instruments. Why did I have such faulty expectations? One reason is that almost nothing was known about Aztec peasants at the time. Before my fieldwork, this gap in our knowledge was filled in, by me and by other Aztec experts, with guesses about those peasants. We all thought these people must have been poor and isolated, dominated and exploited by greedy despotic kings. The results of several years of fieldwork and lab analysis show that this picture was wrong in almost every way.

The bronze sewing needles, my first mystery at Capilco, turned out to be some of the most important finds of these projects. My excavations showed—for Morelos, at least—that bronze was far more abundant and widespread than anyone had imagined. Most middens contained one or two items of bronze. One of the most remarkable things about the bronze objects is that they came from the Tarascan Empire. Not only does this suggest commerce over long distances, but it shows the operation of black-market trade across the fortified Mexica-Tarascan border. So it is not surprising that I consider these small items of bronze the most exciting archaeological finds of my career—that fact alone speaks volumes about the contrast between the approaches of monumental and household archaeology.

The agricultural terraces really should not have been a mystery. It did not take much thought to figure out that if more than a few people were going to live in the Buenavista hills, they needed to build terraces in order to grow enough food in that hilly area of thin, rocky soils. Although excavating terraces was not part of my initial research plans, the decision to focus attention on them was obvious—these terraces are one of the keys to the success of the people of Capilco and Cuexcomate.

The ceramic drum from an excavated rock pile at Cuexcomate was mysterious in two ways. My own lack of knowledge explains my delay in identifying this strange vessel as a drum. But this was only one of several types of musical instruments at these sites, and the bigger mystery was why these supposedly poor and isolated peasants had tossed broken flutes, whistles, and rattles into their middens. Like the bronze needles, these objects signaled the participation of Aztec peasants in wider networks, but they were more religious and cultural in nature than commercial. As a result of these finds, we now know music during rituals was far more widespread in Aztec central Mexico than anyone had thought. These small items indicate something of the diversity and richness of domestic life—that is, a high quality of life—even at the smallest and most provincial Aztec sites. While it would be hard to argue that musical instruments helped people survive and prosper in the ways that terraces or cotton production did, it is not too much of a stretch to see them as one small component of the good life in Aztec-period Morelos.

In our trips to Cuernavaca each year, my family also learned something about the meaning of "the good life" in the U.S. and Mexico today. During our first project, April and Heather experienced rural poverty in the village of Tetlama. In Heather's words, "When nature called, we used the bathroom in the cornfield as there were no indoor facilities. I remember being so excited at one point when an actual toilet was installed over a hole in the ground."

The girls willingly donated their old clothes and toys to their Tetlama friends, whose families struggled to survive day to day. The contrast with the prosperity of their ancestors at Capilco and Cuexcomate was dramatic. But then when we excavated at Yautepec a few years later, April and Heather experienced the opposite end of the Mexican social hierarchy. We were told (incorrectly, it turns out) that as foreigners the girls could not attend public schools, so we found a private bilingual school in Cuernavaca called the "Instituto Oxford." The steep tuition fee was a real strain on my professor's salary, but the school was a good one. Mornings were taught in Spanish and afternoons in English, and April and Heather were each advanced a grade for their afternoon classes.

I think we may have been the poorest family at the Instituto Oxford. The contrast—not just with Tetlama, but with our own middle-class lifestyle in the U.S.—was quite obvious to the kids. Heather recalls:

> My Mexican school friends lived in mansions, with security at the gates of their residences. They had servants, cooks, in-ground pools, private tennis courts, the whole works. Their parents spoke both Spanish and English and regularly flew to Texas to shop. Sleepover parties were a blast with someone else being paid to clean up after us! Experiencing this level of luxury was very different from our modest house with no maid service back in the U.S.

April and Heather would complain that "we are the only ones in school without servants." They insist today that this was just an observation, not a complaint, but I recall it as a typical child's grievance. These experiences among the very poor and the very rich helped shape the girls' personalities. Again, in Heather's words: "Having best friends from complete opposite ends of the socio-economic spectrum made me appreciate people for who they are on the inside." And the experience of being a minority (non-Mexican) while growing up gave April and Heather a level of tolerance and understanding they never forgot.

A new view of Aztec society

One book is not going to erase the view of the Aztecs as sacrificial maniacs. That stereotype is too deeply engrained in popular culture today. Aztec priests did carry out public ceremonies of human sacrifice, although scholars cannot yet determine just how frequent these were. Human sacrifice was not limited to the imperial capital, or even to the Valley of Mexico. Indeed, archaeologist Jorge Angulo excavated a major sacrificial offering (thirty skulls with associated cervical vertebrae) at the site of Teopanzolco in Cuernavaca dating to the Settlement Period (Smith 2008: 35). This find puts a lie to the self-serving claim by a Morelos official, who told Spanish administrators that the people of Morelos did not engage in human sacrifice before the bloodthirsty Mexica conquered them and forced them to carry out these terrible rituals (Acuña 1984–88: vol. 6, p. 186).

Human sacrifice, however, had little influence on daily life. I could find no evidence of the practice, or its byproducts, in domestic deposits. Burial 2 at Yautepec looked at first like the remains of a sacrificial funeral, and I did everything I could to find evidence for sacrifice on the two partially articulated bodies. But they had no cut marks, and the setting, a commoner house, was not the right setting for the sacrificial funerals described for Aztec kings and powerful nobles. The human skull inside two nested pots that a construction worker donated to the project might have been the partial remains of a sacrifice, but I have no idea where it was found, if it was indeed from Yautepec at all.

Historian Inga Clendinnen has speculated that reminders of human sacrifice were ubiquitous in the imperial capital Tenochtitlan and traumatized people in their daily lives (Clendinnen 1991: 68). Whether or not she is correct about the capital, commoners in provincial cities and towns were insulated from sacrificial activities in their daily lives. Sacrifices happened at the central temple-pyramid of the city-state, sponsored by kings and nobles and carried out by high priests. They were the Aztec equivalent of public executions. In large cities, people undoubtedly witnessed the occasional sacrificial ritual, but that was the extent of their involvement.

Another negative view of the Aztecs has more truth to it. Documentary sources mention droughts and famines in the Valley of Mexico during the century before the arrival of Cortés. These accounts have fueled the notion that Aztec agriculture was not productive enough to feed growing populations, and that the expansion of the Mexica Empire was impelled by a desperate drive to find new food sources. While this account might or might not fit the Valley of Mexico (the evidence is equivocal), the situation in Morelos was different. The population did grow throughout the Aztec epoch, with only a minor decline in quality of life in the

Imperial Period. But there is no evidence for famines or other food crises. The households and communities in this area used small-scale intensive agriculture to keep up with their food needs.

Given the reputation of the Aztecs as sacrificial maniacs, imperialists, and starving urbanites, who would have thought that the Mexica Empire was the setting for communities and households that were successful and resilient?

Why were these households and communities successful?

The various lines of evidence from my excavations point to a single conclusion: the communities and households of Capilco, Cuexcomate, and Yautepec were highly successful. These people forged ways of life that allowed them to thrive and prosper. I started to read what social scientists have to say about successful communities today—why are some communities prosperous and healthy while others are not? Based on those works, I came up with four reasons or causes that I believe were responsible for their success: resources, local control, flexible organization, and economic networks. Working against these were two negative forces: overpopulation and exploitation by nobles. In the end, positive forces proved stronger than the negative ones, up until the Spaniards arrived and introduced their new and invincible destructive forces.

Resources

For the Aztec communities of Morelos, two resources stand out: the environmental factors and cultural knowledge that permitted intensive agriculture, and cotton with the technology of textile production. Intensive agricultural methods involve heavy human labor in the field to achieve a high yield of crops on the land. The Morelos households used terracing, irrigation, and kitchen gardens. Without the terraces built at Capilco and Cuexcomate, no more than a few farmers would have been able to survive in this corner of the Buenavista hills.

Yautepec's situation was different. Located at the edge of a rich floodplain, Yautepec and its people could survive easily—at a low population—without intensive agricultural methods. Simple rainfall agriculture works fine in this setting. But by building a system of dams and canals for irrigation they greatly expanded the productivity of the land. This provided the food and cotton that permitted a capital city to flourish and expand. Cotton was the key individual resource in ancient Morelos. Given its use as money—to pay taxes and make purchases in the markets—cotton was a huge boost to the productivity and prosperity of the people of Yautepec. The fact that cotton could not grow in other parts of the central Mexican highlands (because of the altitude) made it even more central to the economic success of the Morelos communities compared to cities without cotton like Calixtlahuaca and Xaltocan.

Morelos provided many other economic resources. I found evidence for tree bark that was made into paper, basalt for *manos* and *metates*, clay for pottery, stone for construction, and limestone to manufacture plaster. But these goods were far less important than intensive agriculture and cotton. The works on contemporary communities remind us that human resources also contribute to community success. Urban planner Sidney Brower notes that in successful communities, coresidents, as a group:

> stand to gain or lose from the actions of individual residents, and individuals stand to gain or lose from the actions of the group. Think of neighborhood improvements that increase the value of an individual property, or of a street that becomes less desirable because a neighbor allows his property to deteriorate.
>
> *(Brower 2011: 6)*

In the sites I excavated, human resources played a crucial role because of their patterns of local control and flexible organization.

Local control

Most things work better when control is in local hands. Common resources such as forests and fisheries are managed more effectively by local users; government decisions about community-level affairs are more efficient and popular when made locally; and local control can make communities and neighborhoods more resilient and sustainable (Bowles and Gintis 2002: F422–F423; McKibben 2007; Ostrom 1990). The economists Bowles and Gintis describe the value of local control—that is, control by communities—like this: "Communities can sometimes do what governments and markets fail to do because their members, but not outsiders, have crucial information about other members' behaviors, capacities, and needs. Members use this information to uphold norms" (Bowles and Gintis 2002: F422–F423).

Several kinds of local control characterized the three Morelos communities. The construction of the terraces at Capilco and Cuexcomate was planned and carried out primarily by households, possibly with help from their *calpolli*. Households mostly farmed the terraces, too, if only because of the frequent but unpredictable need for maintenance on the walls.

Less evidence exists for how irrigation farming was organized at Yautepec. The dams and canals that operate today in the city of Yautepec are technologically simple and they operate on a small scale. In the past, a system like this could easily have been run at the city or neighborhood level.

The prevalence of city-state government in Aztec central Mexico is another example of local control. City-states were small; in Morelos they averaged thirty square miles, with fewer than 10,000 residents. The observations of Bowles and Gintis apply to city-states, but not to the much larger Mexica Empire. Their small size gave city-states an advantage in tailoring policies and actions to local conditions, and they could respond to local issues much more effectively than a larger and more powerful distant state. It was in the interest of the city-state king for his subject communities to flourish, compared to the distant Mexica emperor, who could not care less about provincial communities.

Flexible organization

The ideas of Bowles and Gintis about community success (quoted above) are not just about local control: they also emphasize flexibility. Indeed, flexibility and local control are closely linked: each factor promotes and reinforces the other.

The complexity of household organization in Morelos suggests domestic flexibility. We know about this complexity from the early Spanish census documents. Many households consisted of more than one nuclear family, and unrelated boarders labeled as farm helpers often lived with families. Similar patterns of complex households occur in many peasant societies around the world. Occupants of households change over the seasons and through time in response to the needs of agricultural activity. Landless laborers—who did not belong to a *calpolli*—would have joined prosperous households to help with farm work, and when conditions were tough they could be let go, perhaps to try their fortunes in another region or a larger city.

The *calpolli* had built-in flexibility. The allocation of lands by the council could be adjusted at any time, as could membership. Imbalances in land holdings could be evened out among the member households, and *calpolli* leaders or household heads could recruit new members if they needed more labor.

Wherever we choose to look throughout history, we find the same processes of flexible organization and local control creating success for communities and neighborhoods. To take just one example, historian Cem Behar analyzed documents from a small neighborhood of Istanbul—called Kasap Ilyas—over many centuries:

> This resilience and the physical and social flexibility of our particular city quarter needs explanation, when viewed over a number of centuries. That the small Kasap Ilyas neighborhood had the capacity . . . to absorb rural migrants and integrate newcomers is striking enough. The fact that, in the last four centuries, it has more or less successfully survived a number of devastating fires, earthquakes, political instability, changes in the economic fortunes of Istanbul, and nineteenth-century throes of modernization must be a sign of its power of adaptation.
>
> *(Behar 2003: 10)*

In other words, the people of Kasap Ilyas worked together, largely under the radar of the Ottoman Empire, to create and maintain a successful and prosperous community through bottom-up activities, just as the residents of the excavated sites did in Aztec-period Morelos.

Economic networks

The three forces discussed above—resources, local control, and flexible organization—operated at the local scale, advancing continuity and wealth. But without a good economic connection to the outside world, these communities and households would falter and even collapse. The Aztec market system tied all of central

Mexico and beyond into a single network—it was the main external connection for the people of Morelos. The markets let people sell their raw cotton, textiles, and other goods. And without a steady source of obsidian, salt, bronze, and key ceramic items, the domestic middens would be far poorer than we found them to be.

The importance of economic and social networks for community success today is shown by the research of anthropologist Sandra Wallman. In her book, *The Capability of Places*, she compared a successful and dynamic neighborhood with a declining neighborhood in each of three cities: London, Rome, and Lusaka. In spite of the cultural differences among these cities, all of the successful neighborhoods had effective networks that linked community members to the outside. Some people had moved in from elsewhere, others had employment outside the community, and all of them maintained multiple interactions with the outside world. At the same time, people in the declining neighborhoods had fewer such external connections (Wallman 2011).

The commercial institutions of the Aztec economy—markets, merchants, and money—go a long way toward accounting for the success of the communities and households of Morelos. But it is important to remember that this was not a capitalist economy. This is the point I made in responding to an attack by the Socialist Labor Party in their newspaper, *The People*. Members of this Trotskyite political party didn't like an article I had published on my excavations in *Scientific American* where I talked about markets and merchants (Smith 1997). They attacked me for describing the Aztecs like the cartoon series, *The Flintstones*, where the distant past is filled with all sorts of anachronistic modern features. I was guilty—according to the Socialist Labor Party—of attributing capitalist features to an ancient economy. Therefore, they went on, I must have been implying that capitalism is universal and inevitable. But, as I pointed out in a letter to *The People*, the absence of key features of early capitalism—wage labor, advanced accounting procedures, a market for land—meant that the Aztecs had a *non-capitalist* commercial economy (Smith 2004; Trigger 2003). In fact, one could say that the absence of these features makes the prosperity and success of the Morelos communities all the more remarkable.

The limits of success

If these communities were so successful and resilient, why didn't they survive the Spanish conquest? In fact, many Aztec communities *did* survive and even managed to flourish under Spanish rule. But Morelos was especially hard hit by both European diseases and economic disruptions—more so than other parts of central Mexico. Its lower elevation—and thus its warmer and wetter climate—were more favorable for the spread of diseases such as smallpox and measles than the other central Mexican valleys. And its land soon became the most profitable in central Mexico after the quick changeover of irrigation systems from maize and cotton to sugar cane. But now Spaniards owned the land, and the surviving natives were forced to labor on plantations. The limits of success of the Aztec communities of Morelos became quite clear in the aftermath of the Spanish conquest.

In the five centuries after 1521, circumstances conspired to hold back most of the native communities that did survive the Spanish conquest. These villages were first exploited by the Spaniards for their labor. Within a couple of decades of the conquest, formerly prosperous villages had become settings of poverty and disease. Then after independence from Spain in 1810, capitalist hacienda owners stole their land, often with the tacit support of the federal government. And since the Mexican Revolution in 1910, the national government has regulated peasant villages and their economic activity, not always for their benefit (Carmack et al. 2007; Wolf 1959). This heritage of exploitation contrasts with the local control and flexibility that had permitted the Aztec communities to flourish. Five centuries of change has transformed successful and resilient Aztec communities into poor modern Mexican villages.

Sustainable smallholder agriculture

These Morelos communities are far from unique in their success and prosperity. In his book, *Smallholders, Householders: Farm Families and the Ecology of Intensive, Sustainable Agriculture*, Robert Netting describes a type of rural community whose members have achieved success through some of the same causes that operated in Aztec-period Morelos. Netting compared small-scale peasant communities around the world. He found remarkably similar circumstances in widely diverse settings, from Africa to Switzerland, from Mexico to the Philippines (Netting 1993); see also Wilken (1987) or Whitmore and Turner (2001). The communities I excavated fit right in with Netting's examples, and this comparison helps us understand the significance of Capilco, Cuexcomate, and Yautepec in the world of small-scale farmers.

Netting is careful to show that the successful smallholder farmers he analyzes are a specific type of community found only in certain circumstances. His model does not apply to cases where landlords or bureaucrats closely manage the land, giving peasants little control over their own farms. Netting describes how successful agricultural systems were destroyed, leading to famine and hardship, when communist regimes in China and the Soviet Union replaced smallholder agriculture with state-run farms. In Soviet Russia, farmers on bureaucratic collective farms had few incentives to work hard or innovate. In Communist China, communes, brigades, and work teams drastically reduced the efficiency and productivity of former systems of intensive smallholder agriculture (Netting 1993: 22–24).

The first characteristic of successful smallholder farming is the use of simple technology. Tools and equipment can be made and repaired by the family, who do not need to purchase expensive industrial equipment. Farms are either owned by individual households, or else social customs develop that give farmers long-term access to specific fields. The *calpolli* is a good example of one such custom. Having regular access to the same fields allows peasant farmers to improve their land through terraces, canals, and other features to control water and erosion.

Smallholder farmers live close to their fields, and household members work the fields. Farmers develop intimate knowledge of soils, rainfall, and crops, allowing them to get the most out of their fields. And finally, cultivation is intensive; households invest considerable labor, which leads to high yields on the land. Netting's model of smallholder intensive agriculture fits Aztec-period Morelos quite well. Three of the basic principles I think explain the success of the Morelos communities—resources, local control, and flexibility—are singled out by Netting as responsible for smallholder success in many parts of the world. The fourth reason—economic networks—is more specific to my research setting in Morelos. The prosperity and sustainability of the Morelos households was not a fluke or an accident. It makes good sense when put into Netting's framework of smallholder farmers around the world.

A new archaeology of households and communities

Many people think archaeology is about finding treasure. Archaeologists regularly deny that this is so, but it remains a deeply held view in Mexico. "Treasure stories" abound in Mexican folklore, often telling of how someone found Aztec gold or perhaps coins buried during the Mexican Revolution of 1910. When I was a graduate student excavating for Ken Hirth at Xochicalco, my crew had one young worker who refused to believe that broken artifacts were the true target of the excavations. We must be searching for Motecuhzoma's lost gold treasure. Hirth obtained a piece of iron pyrite, known as "fool's gold" for its resemblance to gold, and we planted it where this worker would be sure to find it. Everyone had a good laugh at his look of amazement as he uncovered the pyrite.

One summer in Cuernavaca we hired an out-of-work political cartoonist, Omar Trujillo, to help sort sherds. Omar was friends with one of our regular lab workers. He drew a cartoon of Cindy and me, showing how our excavations *really* worked (Figure 8.1). I am running around clueless with my treasure map and magnifying glass. Meanwhile, Cindy has already found the buried treasure chest on her own. Although the idea of Cindy making important finds while my head is in the clouds may be on the mark, we've never encountered a buried chest of gold.

While we can laugh at the crude idea that archaeology is about finding buried treasure, there is a far more prevalent—and correct—view that archaeology is about fancy objects, tombs, and monumental buildings. This was certainly the focus of the earliest archaeologists, and "monumental archaeology" is still what you will see in television programs on ancient Egypt or the Maya. In contrast, I have tried to show that archaeological fieldwork can produce a richly detailed picture of domestic activities, daily life, and community conditions in the past. I have said little about pyramids, tombs, and kings. Household archaeology starts with the goal of understanding life in the past, particularly among a society's non-elite members. Monumental archaeology, on the other hand, starts with the goal of bringing to light the finest artistic and architectural achievements of ancient societies.

My emphasis on household archaeology dictated many of the methods described in earlier chapters, including random sampling, screening the dirt and quantifying all excavated artifacts, and chemical tests of the soil. Indeed this approach led me to

FIGURE 8.1 Cartoon showing Cindy finding the buried treasure while I am clueless. Drawing by Omar Trujillo; reproduced with permission.

excavate the middens, or trash deposits, located out behind most houses. For those of us who focus on households, a trash heap is more exciting than a tomb.

A different kind of contrast between monumental and household archaeology involves the timing of the moment of archaeological discovery. In the former approach the major finds come during fieldwork: things like the opening of a tomb or the discovery of a new hieroglyphic inscription. But when excavating the middens of ancient peasant farmers, excitement rarely reveals itself in the field—the houses are similar and the middens all look pretty much the same. The important discoveries come later, in the laboratory stage of research. The artifacts tell the stories of what people were doing and who they were.

Archaeologists can still learn much from the temples and tombs of ancient civilizations, whether Aztec, Maya, Sumerian, or Egyptian. I do not want to denigrate monumental archaeology or suggest that it should not be pursued. And I certainly wouldn't throw away a buried treasure chest if I found one in a midden! But now archaeology can do far more by looking at the past in social terms. The sites we map and excavate are the remains of ancient communities whose households struggled to create ways of life that could be successful and sustainable. Even in Aztec Mexico.

How does this story of positive and negative developments in one corner of the Mexica Empire help us understand communities and households in other areas and other times? My answer begins with the Urban Revolution.

The Aztecs and the Urban Revolution

For most of the human past our ancestors lived in small groups, hunting and gathering their food and moving from one temporary campsite to another. After the invention of agriculture—between 10,000 and 2,000 years ago, depending on the area—people in some regions settled down. Villages remained small and, compared to later developments, uncomplicated.

Then came the most dramatic social transformation in the entire human career, the Urban Revolution. This phrase refers not just to the origin of cities, but to the start of state-level societies with kings, laws, taxes, social inequality, specialized economies, and cities. We live in state-level societies today, and our institutions have much in common with those of the Aztecs, Mayas, Greeks, and Egyptians. If we could be transported back in time, most of us would be utterly confused and dismayed to find ourselves in a society before the Urban Revolution, whereas if we landed in Babylon, Athens, or Teotihuacan, conditions would not seem nearly so strange.

The early civilizations were the societies that created the Urban Revolution and flourished in its aftermath. Although these societies set the course of human development for thousands of years, they remain poorly understood today. Erroneous stereotypes plague our understanding of these societies. To take just one example, many people think that all early kings were powerful and egotistical despots who ruled with an iron hand, exploiting the common people who were little better than slaves. Few archaeologists would use this language, but we employ technical-sounding terminology that says the same thing. For me, the face of actor Yul Brynner, playing the Pharaoh Ramses in the film *The Ten Commandments*, comes to mind here.

I freely admit my own guilt in believing this caricature when I started excavating sites in Morelos, and it accounts for some of my puzzlement at the mysteries discussed in Chapter 1. The results described in this book, however, are hard to reconcile with the picture of oppressive kings. The people who lived in the houses I excavated were prosperous, and the *calpolli* and other institutions gave them a good degree of control over their own lives. This book joins work by other archaeologists who are trying to dismantle this and other erroneous stereotypes about the ancient civilizations (e.g., Blanton and Fargher 2008; Earle 1997; Trigger 2003).

Perhaps the major lesson these early civilizations can teach us today is that over the ages people have worked out many different ways to organize their state-level societies. The current international system of nation-states is not the only way societies can be organized, and the Western historical path is not the only viable trajectory of development and change. Some ancient civilizations, such as Egypt and the Inca, thrived under state-controlled economies, while others, like Rome and China, developed advanced commercial economies that resembled capitalism.

The Aztec economy falls somewhere in the middle. Some ancient states really did have powerful autocratic kings—for example, Egypt and Assyria—but others like Greece and Rome allowed significant input from the people in questions of government. Perhaps better understanding these variations can help us think more effectively about our economic and political options today.

Political philosophers frequently look to ancient Greece and Rome for illustrations without considering that ancient New World peoples might have something useful to offer. Sociologists tend to generalize about "society" while ignoring cases like the Aztecs and Incas. The ancient Native American peoples of the New World fashioned innumerable successful, creative societies. And the Aztecs and their ancient American neighbors can provide modern thinkers with a broader base of knowledge from which to explore human issues.

The kind of archaeology described in this book—a social approach focused on households and communities—can uncover reliable information about past social patterns and processes. Those of us who follow this approach are not content to excavate buildings and artifacts for their own sake. Instead, we use our finds to reconstruct ancient societies in terms that can be compared to other societies around the world, past and present. From this perspective, I believe archaeology can offer useful lessons for the present and the future (Sabloff 2008; Smith et al. 2012). Not surprisingly, the major lessons of the Morelos sites lie at the level of the community.

Lessons for communities today

There is no shortage of advice about what communities can do to be successful today. From the perspective of deep history, however, much of that advice sounds shallow and superficial. For example, the Sonoran Institute organization "Western Lands and Communities" offers advice based on a series of "Hallmarks of Successful Communities." These include the provision that successful communities "understand that natural and cultural assets influence and are affected by population growth and development" (https://sustainablecities.asu.edu/docs/SCN/9-22-11/WLC_SCOTie_10-19-11.pdf). A list of seven "Blueprint principles" offered by the Georgia Conservancy claims that successful communities "work together to produce a high quality of life that can be sustained" and that they "promote efficient use of existing infrastructure, land, energy supplies and water" (see http://www.georgiaconservancy.org/blueprints/blueprints-principles.html). These are platitudes, not useful advice.

Unlike these vague precepts, one can apply the principles of success and prosperity from Chapters 4 and 7 to examine patterns of successful and failed communities over long periods of time. In this book I have told the stories of three communities that lasted for many centuries while providing a high level of prosperity for their residents. Although the Aztec sites offer few pieces of direct advice to modern communities, a number of observations do have relevance for understanding the modern world.

1 Small is beautiful: appropriate technology can get the job done

The kinds of smallholder farming practiced in Aztec-period Morelos—terracing and irrigation—are examples of what is known as small-scale or appropriate technology. The appropriate technology movement began in the 1960s with economist E. F. Schumacher's book *Small is Beautiful*. Schumacher advocated small-scale technology as a viable option for improving life in India and other developing nations. It works because it relies mainly on human labor, whether foot-powered water pumps or bicycle-based urban transport methods. Appropriate technology is organized on a local scale and often employs traditional knowledge (Schumacher 1975).

Schumacher's argument is the technological counterpart to Netting's model of smallholder agriculture. Small-scale agricultural methods and technology have often proved more successful in stimulating economic activity in developing nations today than methods of large-scale industrialized farming that rely on heavy machinery and petrochemicals that peasant farmers just cannot afford. Likewise, small business loans ("microfinance") have contributed enormously to the economic success of thousands of small-scale business owners and entrepreneurs in the developing world today.

Archaeologist Clark Erickson had an active role in re-introducing an ancient intensive agricultural method—known as raised fields—in Peru. Erickson had excavated ancient examples of these features, and he taught local farmers how to build and farm them. This was partly an exercise in experimental archaeology—to learn how such fields were constructed and used—but it quickly turned into a small-scale economic development project. The local people did not have the capital to buy the tractors, the expensive hybrid seeds, and the petrochemicals needed for modern industrial farming. But they did have abundant personnel and the traditional customs of household and community labor that allowed appropriate or smallholder agriculture to flourish (Erickson 1989, 2003).[1]

The long-term sustainability of terrace and irrigation agriculture in Aztec-period Morelos furnishes a model for communities in the developing world. Smallholder agriculture, done with simple technology, can flourish and provide support for communities, even in marginal environments like the Buenavista hills.

2 Choose the right connections

The external world impinges on families and households in many ways, and people rarely have the freedom to simply choose how to interact with governments, markets, and other external institutions. Nevertheless, just about any household in the world today has a suite of external connections available to its members. Once the mandatory connections are taken care of (for example, by paying taxes and bills), people typically have the option to emphasize or de-emphasize various social connections. A growing body of research shows that such networks often provide the key to individual and family prosperity and success (Sampson 2004; Watts 2004). For example, Charles Tilly has shown that the standard folk explanation for why some poor people in the developing world achieve economic success—hard work and virtue—is misleading because in many cases individual success owes more to social connections and networks than to hard work or virtue (Tilly 2007).

The external connections of the Morelos households shaped their destiny. By focusing their social networks at the local scale, through the household and *calpolli*, commoners managed to insulate themselves from the negative effects of Aztec conquest. They had to pay the new imperial taxes, of course. But smallholder agriculture and a local orientation allowed them to produce enough cotton textiles to absorb these taxes without damage to the local economy or society. At the same time people participated heavily in the market system, which was one of the strongest forces generating economic prosperity in this region.

By using the markets effectively, the residents of Capilco, Cuexcomate, and Yautepec managed to "choose the right connections," balancing local concerns with more distant forces. This allowed them to create the continuity and prosperity of a successful way of life. It is not too far-fetched to suggest that the suite of external connections used by modern communities can have major effects on their prosperity and success.

3 Local control and flexibility lead to success

Local control and organizational flexibility, at both the household and community levels, were major reasons for the long-term success of the Morelos communities. This finding makes sense in terms of current research on the importance of communities in social, political, and economic life. Today, when Walmart arrives in a town, local stores are put out of business and the community suffers. This is one of Bill McKibben's reasons—in his book *Deep Economy: The Wealth of Communities and the Durable Future* (2007)—for advocating a return to local economies and local decision-making. The emphasis on local control is a big part of McKibben's path to more livable communities and a more sustainable future. Community experts John McKnight and Peter Block also emphasize the value of local control and flexibility. They point to features like farmer's markets and the local food movement, or joint labor to improve public spaces such as parks and playgrounds (McKnight 2013; McKnight and Block 2010).

But the value of local control goes far beyond the modern developed world. Political scientist Elinor Ostrom was awarded the 2009 Nobel Prize in Economics for showing how traditional village communities have long regulated common-pool resources (such as forests, irrigation systems, and fisheries) in ways that are both more efficient and more sustainable than either markets (privatization) or governments (state ownership). Local communities can accomplish this because they are the settings for considerable face-to-face interaction. The use of resources can be monitored, and outsiders can be excluded (Bowles and Gintis 2002; Ostrom 1990). Most of the cases analyzed by Ostrom

> are small-scale village societies in the developing world. Practices and customs developed by these communities allow resources to be managed efficiently for the benefit of the entire community. The phrase "Local control and flexibility lead to success" could be a summary of the results of her research.
>
> Elinor Ostrom's findings were extended further by economists Bowles and Gintis. They have shown how traditional and contemporary communities can solve many problems of coordinated action and cooperation. Their central insight—that communities are able to accomplish things that markets and government cannot do alone—fits with the idea that civic virtue consists of people working together to solve their common problems.

The fact that my results from Aztec-period Morelos correspond to what is known about communities and cooperation in the modern world might sound strange at first. After all, the economic, technological, and political gaps between the Aztecs and the modern world are dramatic. But what this comparison shows is that the importance and strength of local communities is something that transcends the divide between ancient and modern society.

Note

1 At one point, before starting the Yautepec project, I tried to get funding to carry out a similar project in Morelos. An agronomist in Cuernavaca wanted to re-introduce small-scale terracing as a viable agricultural method today, and we planned to excavate more Aztec-period terraces for details about how the ancient system had worked. But for various reasons we failed to find funding, and the project never got off the ground.

REFERENCES

Acuña, René (1984–88) *Relaciones geográficas del siglo XVI*. 10 vols. Universidad Nacional Autónoma de México, Mexico City.

Adger, W. Neil (2000) Social and Ecological Resilience: Are They Related? *Progress in Human Geography* 24: 347–364.

Andrews, Bradford W. (2008) Stone Tools in Mesoamerica: Flaked Stone Tools. In *Encyclopaedia of the History of Science, Technology, and Medicine in Non-Wesern Cultures, revised Internet edition*, edited by Helaine Selin, pp. 2029–2042. 2nd edn, vol. 2. Springer, Dordrecht.

Behar, Cem (2003) *A Neighborhood in Ottoman Istanbul: Fruit Vendors and Civil Servants in the Kasap {I}lyas* Mahalle. State University of New York Press, Albany, NY.

Belcher, John C. (1951) Evaluation and Restandardization of Sewell's Socio-Economic Scale. *Rural Sociology* 16: 246–255.

Berdan, Frances F. (1987) Cotton in Aztec Mexico: Production, Distribution, and Uses. *Mexican Studies/Estudios Mexicanos* 3: 235–262.

—— (2005) *The Aztecs of Central Mexico: An Imperial Society*. 2nd edn. Thomson-Wadsworth, Belmont, CA.

—— (2014) *Aztec Archaeology and Ethnohistory*. Cambridge University Press, New York.

Berdan, Frances F. and Patricia R. Anawalt (eds) (1992) *The Codex Mendoza*. 4 vols. University of California Press, Berkeley.

Blanton, Richard E. and Lane F. Fargher (2008) *Collective Action in the Formation of Pre-Modern States*. Springer, New York.

Both, Arnd Adje (2002) Aztec Flower Flutes: The Symbolic Organization of Sound in Late Postclassic Mesoamerica. *Orient-Archäologie* 10: 279–289.

—— (2007) Aztec Music Culture. In *Music Archaeology: Mesoamerica*, edited by Max Peter Baumann, Arnd Adje Both, and Julia L. J. Sanchez, pp. 91–194. *The World of Music*, vol. 49 (2). University of Bamberg, Bamberg.

Bowles, Samuel and Herbert Gintis (2002) Social Capital and Community Governance. *The Economic Journal* 112 (483): F419–F436.

Brower, Sidney N. (2011) *Neighbors and Neighborhoods: Elements of Successful Community Design*. APA Planners Press, Chicago.

Brumfiel, Elizabeth M. (1980) Specialization, Market Exchange, and the Aztec State: A View From Huexotla. *Current Anthropology* 21: 459–478.
Carballo, David M. (2011) Advances in the Household Archaeology of Highland Mesoamerica. *Journal of Archaeological Research* 19: 133–189.
Carmack, Robert M., Janine Gasco, and Gary H. Gossen (eds) (2007) *The Legacy of Mesoamerica: History and Culture of a Native American Civilization.* 2nd edn. Prentice-Hall, Englewood Cliffs, NJ.
Carrasco, Pedro (1976) The Joint Family in Ancient Mexico: The Case of Molotla. In *Essays on Mexican Kinship*, edited by Hugo Nutini, Pedro Carrasco, and James M. Taggert, pp. 45–64. University of Pittsburgh Press, Pittsburgh.
Charlton, Thomas H., Deborah L. Nichols, and Cynthia L. Otis Charlton (2000) Otumba and its Neighbors: Ex Oriente Lux. *Ancient Mesoamerica* 11: 247–266.
Clendinnen, Inga (1991) *Aztecs: An Interpretation.* Cambridge University Press, New York.
Cline, S. L. (1993) *The Book of Tributes: Early Sixteenth-Century Nahuatl Censuses from Morelos.* U.C.L.A. Latin American Center, Los Angeles.
Congress for the New Urbanism (2008) "Canons of Sustainable Architecture and Urbanism: A Companion to the Charter for the New Urbanism," Congress for the New Urbanism. https://www.cnu.org/charter-new-urbanism/canons-sustainable-architecture-and-urbanism.
Cowgill, George L. (2015) *Ancient Teotihuacan: Early Urbanism in Central Mexico.* Cambridge University Press, New York.
Curtis, Daniel R. (2014) *Coping with Crisis: The Resilience and Vulnerability of Pre-Industrial Settlements.* Ashgate, Farnham.
Dempsey, Nicola, Glen Bramley, Sinéad Power, and Caroline Brown (2011) The Social Dimension of Sustainable Development: Defining Urban Social Sustainability. *Sustainable Development* 19: 289–300.
Díaz del Castillo, Bernal (1963) *The Conquest of New Spain.* Translated by J. M. Cohen. Penguin, New York.
Dodds Pennock, Caroline (2008) *Bonds of Blood: Gender, Lifecycle, and Sacrifice in Aztec Culture.* Palgrave, London.
Earle, Timothy (1997) *How Chiefs Come to Power: The Political Economy in Prehistory.* Stanford University Press, Stanford.
Elson, Christina M. and Michael E. Smith (2001) Archaeological Deposits from the Aztec New Fire Ceremony. *Ancient Mesoamerica* 12: 157–174.
Erickson, Clark L. (1989) Raised Field Agriculture in the Lake Titicaca Basin: Putting Ancient Agriculture Back to Work. *Expedition* 30 (3): 8–16.
—— (2003) Agricultural Landscapes as World Heritage: Raised Field Agriculture in Bolivia and Peru. In *Managing Change: Sustainable Approaches to the Conservation of the Built Environment*, edited by Jeanne-Marie Teutonica and Frank Matero, pp. 181–204. Getty Conservation Institute, Los Angeles.
Flannery, Kent V. (ed.) (1976) *The Early Mesoamerican Village.* Academic Press, New York.
Flint, J. (2009) Neighborhoods and Community. In *International Encyclopedia of Human Geography*, edited by Rob Kitchin and Nigel Thrift, pp. 354–359, vol. 7. Elsevier, Oxford.
Garraty, Christopher P. and Barbara L. Stark (eds) (2010) *Archaeological Approaches to Market Exchange in Ancient Societies.* University Press of Colorado, Boulder.
Gerring, John, Daniel Ziblatt, Johan van Gorp, and Julián Arévalo (2011) An Institutional Theory of Direct and Indirect Rule. *World Politics* 63 (3): 377–433.
Glaeser, Edward L. (2011) *The Triumph of Cities: How our Greatest Invention Makes us Richer, Smarter, Greener, Healthier, and Happier.* Penguin, New York.

Hanson, Susan (2005) Perspectives on the Geographic Stability and Mobility of People in Cities. *Proceedings of the National Academy of Sciences of the United States of America* 102 (43): 15301–15306.

Hare, Timothy S. and Michael E. Smith (1996) A New Postclassic Chronology for Yautepec, Morelos. *Ancient Mesoamerica* 7: 281–297.

Helferich, Gerard (2011) *Stone of Kings: In Search of the Lost Jade of the Maya*. Lyons Press, New York.

Hirth, Kenneth G. (1998) The Distributional Approach: A New Way to Identify Marketplace Exchange in the Archaeological Record. *Current Anthropology* 39: 451–476.

—— (2000) *Archaeological Research at Xochicalco. Volume 1, Ancient Urbanism at Xochicalco: The Evolution and Organization of a Pre-Hispanic Society. Volume 2, The Xochicalco Mapping Project*. 2 vols. University of Utah Press, Salt Lake City.

Hosler, Dorothy (1994) *The Sounds and Colors of Power: The Sacred Metallurgical Technology of Ancient West Mexico*. MIT Press, Cambridge.

Hosler, Dorothy and Andrew Macfarlane (1996) Copper Sources, Metal Production and Metals Trade in Late Postclassic Mesoamerica. *Science* 273: 1819–1824.

Jennings, Gary (1980) *Aztec*. Avon Books, New York.

Layard, Richard (2006) *Happiness: Lessons from a New Science*. Penguin, New York.

León-Portilla, Miguel (1963) *Aztec Thought and Culture: A Study of the Ancient Náhuatl Mind*. University of Oklahoma Press, Norman.

Lockhart, James (1992) *The Nahuas After the Conquest: A Social and Cultural History of the Indians of Central Mexico, Sixteenth Through Eighteenth Centuries*. Stanford University Press, Stanford.

López Luján, Leonardo (2005) *The Offerings of the Templo Mayor of Tenochtitlan*. Revised ed. Translated by Bernard R. Ortiz de Montellano and Thelma Ortiz de Montellano. University of New Mexico Press, Albuquerque.

Mata-Míguez, Jaime, Lisa Overholtzer, Enrique Rodríguez-Alegría, Brian M. Kemp, and Deborah A. Bolnick (2012) Genetic Impact of Aztec Imperialism: Ancient Mitochondrial DNA Evidence from Xaltocan, Mexico. *American Journal of Physical Anthropology* 149: 504–516.

Matos Moctezuma, Eduardo (1995) *Life and Death in the Templo Mayor*. Translated by Bernard R. Ortiz de Montellano and Thelma Ortiz de Montellano. University Press of Colorado, Boulder.

McCaa, Robert (2003) The Nahua Calli of Ancient Mexico: Household, Family, and Gender. *Continuity and Change* 18: 23–48.

McKibben, Bill (2007) *Deep Economy: The Wealth of Communities and the Durable Future*. Henry Holt, New York.

McKnight, John (2013) Neighborhood Necessities: Seven Functions that Only Effectively Organized Neighborhoods Can Provide. *National Civic Review* 102 (3): 22–24.

McKnight, John and Peter Block (2010) *The Abundant Community: Awakening the Power of Families and Neighborhoods*. Berrett-Koehler, San Francisco.

Millon, René, R. Bruce Drewitt, and George L. Cowgill (1973) *Urbanization at Teotihuacan, Mexico, Volume 1: The Teotihuacan Map, Part 2: Maps*. University of Texas Press, Austin.

Mintz, Sidney W. and Eric R. Wolf (1950) An Analysis of Ritual Co-Parenthood (*Compadrazgo*). *Southwestern Journal of Anthropology* 6: 341–368.

Morehart, Christopher T. (2012) Mapping Ancient Chinampa Landscapes in the Basin of Mexico: A Remote Sensing and GIS Approach. *Journal of Archaeological Science* 39 (7): 2541–2551.

Netting, Robert McC. (1993) *Smallholders, Householders: Farm Families and the Ecology of Intensive, Sustainable Agriculture*. Stanford University Press, Stanford.

Netting, Robert McC., Richard R. Wilk, and Eric J. Arnould (eds) (1984) *Households: Comparative and Historical Studies of the Domestic Group*. University of California Press, Berkeley.
Ostrom, Elinor (1990) *Governing the Commons: The Evolution of Institutions for Collective Action*. Cambridge University Press, New York.
—— (2009) A General Framework for Analyzing Sustainability of Social-Ecological Systems. *Science* 325: 419–422.
Phillips, David (2006) *Quality of Life: Concept, Policy and Practice*. Routledge, New York.
Putnam, Robert D. (2000) *Bowling Alone: The Collapse and Revival of Community in America*. Simon and Schuster, New York.
Rojas, José Luis de (2012) *Tenochtitlan: Capital of the Aztec Empire*. University Press of Florida, Gainesville.
Sabloff, Jeremy A. (2008) *Archaeology Matters: Action Archaeology in the Modern World*. Left Coast Press, Walnut Creek, CA.
Sahagún, Fray Bernardino de (1950–82) *Florentine Codex, General History of the Things of New Spain. 12 books. Translated and Edited by Arthur J. O. Anderson and Charles E. Dibble*. School of American Research and the University of Utah Press, Santa Fe and Salt Lake City.
Sampson, Robert J. (2004) Networks and Neighbourhoods: The Implications of Connectivity for Thinking about Crime in the Modern City. In *Network Logic: Who Governs in an Interconnected World?*, edited by Helen McCarthy, Paul Miller, and Paul Skidmore, pp. 157–166. Demos, London.
—— (2012) *Great American City: Chicago and the Enduring Neighborhood Effect*. University of Chicago Press, Chicago.
Sanborn, Alan F. and Maxine S. Heath (2012) *The Cicadas (Hemiptera: Cicadoidea: Cicadae) of North America North of Mexico*. Entomological Society of America, Lanham, MD.
Schieman, Scott (2005) Residential Stability and the Social Impact of Neighborhood Disadvantage: A Study of Gender- and Race-Contingent Effects. *Social Forces* 83 (3): 1031–1064.
Schumacher, E. F. (1975) *Small is Beautiful: Economics as if People Mattered*. Harper and Row, New York.
Sen, Amartya K. (1992) *Inequality Reexamined*. Russell Sage Foundation, New York.
—— (1999) *Development as Freedom*. Alfred Knopf, New York.
Sewell, William H. (1940) *The Construction and Standardization of a Scale for the Measurement of the Socio-Economic Status of Oklahoma Farm Families*. Technical Bulletin, vol. 9. Oklahoma Agricultural and Mechanical College, Agricultural Exerimental Station, Stillwater, OK.
Smith, Michael E. (1987) Household Possessions and Wealth in Agrarian States: Implications for Archaeology. *Journal of Anthropological Archaeology* 6: 297–335.
—— (1992) *Archaeological Research at Aztec-Period Rural Sites in Morelos, Mexico. Volume 1, Excavations and Architecture/Investigaciones arqueológicas en sitios rurales de la época Azteca en Morelos, Tomo 1, excavaciones y arquitectura*. Memoirs in Latin American Archaeology, vol. 4. University of Pittsburgh, Pittsburgh.
—— (1993) Houses and the Settlement Hierarchy in Late Postclassic Morelos: A Comparison of Archaeology and Ethnohistory. In *Prehispanic Domestic Units in Western Mesoamerica: Studies of the Household, Compound, and Residence*, edited by Robert S. Santley and Kenneth G. Hirth, pp. 191–206. CRC Press, Boca Raton.
—— (1997) Life in the Provinces of the Aztec Empire. *Scientific American* 277 (3): 56–63.
—— (2001) The Aztec World of Gary Jennings. In *Novel History: Historians and Novelists Confront America's Past (and Each Other)*, edited by Mark C. Carnes, pp. 95–105. Simon and Schuster, New York.

—— (2002) Domestic Ritual at Aztec Provincial Sites in Morelos. In *Domestic Ritual in Ancient Mesoamerica*, edited by Patricia Plunket, pp. 93–114. Monograph, vol. 46. Cotsen Institute of Archaeology, UCLA, Los Angeles.

—— (2004) The Archaeology of Ancient State Economies. *Annual Review of Anthropology* 33: 73–102.

—— (2008) *Aztec City-State Capitals*. University Press of Florida, Gainesville.

—— (2012) *The Aztecs*. 3rd edn. Blackwell Publishers, Oxford.

—— (2014) The Aztecs Paid Taxes, not Tribute. *Mexicon* 36 (1): 19–22.

—— (2015a) *Artefactos Domésticos de Casas Posclásicas en Cuexcomate y Capilco, Morelos*. BAR International Series, vol. 2696. Archaeopress, Oxford.

—— (2015b) The Aztec Empire. In *Fiscal Regimes and the Political Economy of Premodern States*, edited by Andrew Monson and Walter Scheidel, pp. 71–114. Cambridge University Press, New York.

—— (2016a) *Excavaciones de Casas en la Ciudad Azteca de Yautepec, Morelos, México*. BAR International Series. Archaeopress, Oxford.

—— (2016b) Quality of Life and Prosperity in Ancient Households and Communities. In *The Oxford Handbook of Historical Ecology and Applied Archaeology*, edited by Christian Isendahl and Daryl Stump. Oxford University Press, New York.

Smith, Michael E., Aleksander Borejsza, Angela Huster, Charles D. Frederick, Isabel Rodríguez López, and Cynthia Heath-Smith (2013) Aztec-Period Houses and Terraces at Calixtlahuaca: The Changing Morphology of a Mesoamerican Hilltop Urban Center. *Journal of Field Archaeology* 38 (3): 227–243.

Smith, Michael E. and John F. Doershuk (1991) Late Postclassic Chronology in Western Morelos, Mexico. *Latin American Antiquity* 2: 291–310.

Smith, Michael E., Gary M. Feinman, Robert D. Drennan, Timothy Earle, and Ian Morris (2012) Archaeology as a Social Science. *Proceedings of the National Academy of Sciences* 109: 7617–7621.

Smith, Michael E., Cynthia Heath-Smith, Ronald Kohler, Joan Odess, Sharon Spanogle, and Timothy Sullivan (1994) The Size of the Aztec City of Yautepec: Urban Survey in Central Mexico. *Ancient Mesoamerica* 5: 1–11.

Smith, Michael E., Cynthia Heath-Smith, and Lisa Montiel (1999) Excavations of Aztec Urban Houses at Yautepec, Mexico. *Latin American Antiquity* 10: 133–150.

Smith, Michael E. and Kenneth G. Hirth (1988) The Development of Prehispanic Cotton-Spinning Technology in Western Morelos, Mexico. *Journal of Field Archaeology* 15: 349–358.

Smith, Michael E., Juliana Novic, Angela Huster, and Peter C. Kroefges (2009) Reconocimiento superficial y mapeo en Calixtlahuaca. *Expresión Antropológica* 36: 39–55.

Smith, Michael E. and T. Jeffrey Price (1994) Aztec-Period Agricultural Terraces in Morelos, Mexico: Evidence for Household-Level Agricultural Intensification. *Journal of Field Archaeology* 21: 169–179.

Stiglitz, Joseph E., Amartya Sen, and Jean-Paul Fitoussi (2010) *Mismeasuring Our Lives: Why GDP Doesn't Add Up*. The New Press, New York.

Tainter, Joseph A. and Temis G. Taylor (2014) Complexity, Problem-Solving, Sustainability and Resilience. *Building Research and Information* 42 (2): 168–181.

Tarkanian, Michael J. and Dorothy Hosler (2011) American's First Polymer Scientists: Rubber Processing, Use and Transport in Mesoamerica. *Latin American Antiquity* 22 (4): 469–486.

Tilly, Charles (1985) War Making and State Making as Organized Crime. In *Bringing the State Back in*, edited by Peter Evans, Dietrich Rueschmeyer, and Theda Skocpol, pp. 169–186. Cambridge University Press, New York.

—— (2007) Poverty and the Politics of Exclusion. In *Moving Out of Poverty, Volume 1: Cross-Disciplinary Perspectives on Mobility*, edited by Deepa Narayan-Parker and Patti Petesch, pp. 45–76. World Bank, Washington, DC.

Townsend, Richard F. (2009) *The Aztecs*. 3rd edn. Thames and Hudson, New York.

Trigger, Bruce G. (2003) *Understanding Early Civilizations: A Comparative Study*. Cambridge University Press, New York.

Wallman, Sandra (2011) *The Capability of Places: Methods for Modelling Community Response to Intrusion and Change*. Pluto Press, London.

Ward, Peter M. (1978) Social Interaction Patterns in Squatter Settlements in Mexico City. *Geoforum* 9: 235–243.

Watts, Duncan J. (2004) *Six Degrees: The Science of a Connected Age*. Norton, New York.

Whitmore, Thomas M. and B. L. Turner, II (2001) *Cultivated Landscapes of Middle America on the Eve of Conquest*. Oxford University Press, New York.

Wilk, Richard R. and Wendy Ashmore (eds) (1988) *Household and Community in the Mesoamerican Past*. University of New Mexico Press, Albuquerque.

Wilken, Gene C. (1987) *Good Farmers: Traditional Agricultural Resource Management in Mexico and Central America*. University of California Press, Berkeley.

Wilkinson, Richard G. (1998) *Skeletal Analysis of the Yautepec Burials*. Yautepec Project, University at Albany, SUNY, Albany.

Wolf, Eric R. (1959) *Sons of the Shaking Earth*. University of Chicago Press, Chicago.

Wylie, Alison (1985) The Reaction Against Analogy. *Advances in Archaeological Method and Theory* 8: 63–111.

INDEX